LEADERSHIP AWARENESS AND DEVELOPMENT PROGRAM

Instructional Guide

Russell L. Kaiser

BALBOA.
PRESS
A DIVISION OF HAY HOUSE

This book is a work of non-fiction. Unless otherwise noted, the author and the publisher make no explicit guarantees as to the accuracy of the information contained in this book and in some cases, names of people and places have been altered to protect their privacy.

Balboa Press books may be ordered through booksellers or by contacting:

Balboa Press
A Division of Hay House
1663 Liberty Drive
Bloomington, IN 47403
www.balboapress.com
1 (877) 407-4847

Because of the dynamic nature of the Internet, any web addresses or links contained in this book may have changed since publication and may no longer be valid. The views expressed in this work are solely those of the author and do not necessarily reflect the views of the publisher, and the publisher hereby disclaims any responsibility for them.

The author of this book does not dispense medical advice or prescribe the use of any technique as a form of treatment for physical, emotional, or medical problems without the advice of a physician, either directly or indirectly. The intent of the author is only to offer information of a general nature to help you in your quest for emotional and spiritual well-being. In the event you use any of the information in this book for yourself, which is your constitutional right, the author and the publisher assume no responsibility for your actions.

Any people depicted in stock imagery provided by Getty Images are models, and such images are being used for illustrative purposes only.
Certain stock imagery © Getty Images.

Print information available on the last page.

ISBN: 978-1-9822-1036-6 (sc)
ISBN: 978-1-9822-1037-3 (e)

Balboa Press rev. date: 08/29/2018

CONTENTS

Part 2: Program Support

Note: This table of contents could also serve as the program table of contents.

PREFACE

After I'd had the opportunity to participate in several beginning and intermediate leadership development programs, my previous boss with the US Army Corps of Engineers challenged me to develop a basic-level leadership program for the Savannah district. I accepted the challenge.

I first went to the literature to identify the different types of programs that had been previously developed and published. In my search, I did not find any resource document that I could use as an instructional guide. Therefore, I built a program based on what I'd learned in leadership development courses I'd taken throughout my twenty-five-plus-year career; on what I'd learned over my lifetime; on what I expected from my leaders; and on insights I'd gained by talking with other senior leaders inside and outside of my organization.

The most notable programs and courses that I have taken to date include the following:

- Office of Personnel Management's (OPM) Leadership for a Democratic Society
- Army Management Staff College Intermediate Leadership Program
- Executive Communications
- Senior Executive Assessment Program
- Budget
- Conflict Management and Dispute Resolution
- Leadership and Development
- Lead

I am also an instructor for employing and discussing the Strength Deployment Inventory by Elias H. Porter, PhD.

I developed my first program and presented the curriculum to the other senior leaders in the Savannah district. The program was approved, and I facilitated the course for the first two years. After completion of the first year, I refined the program based on feedback from the students and personal reflection. This experience was an incredible opportunity for me, as it allowed me to participate in helping young leaders grow in their journey while advancing my own personal leadership journey.

Shortly after I joined the US Environmental Protection Agency (EPA), there was an organizational 360-review performed on the management team in the Office of Wetlands, Oceans, and Watersheds (OWOW). In part, we found that staff had a low morale because there were few advancement opportunities and few opportunities to increase their leadership skills. I proposed to the senior leaders that I develop a leadership program for the OWOW. As a base model, I used the refined program that I had developed for the Savannah district. I updated the program based on additional advanced coursework that I had taken via the OPM. After attending the Federal Executive Institute, Leadership for a Democratic Society, I made additional modifications to the program. The revised program is presented herein.

As a result of the many benefits I have gained by developing and implementing a Leadership Awareness and Development Program (LADP), and knowing that few resources are available for creating program proposals, I wanted to put forth a practical instructional tool that could guide others who are in a similar position as I was and are interested in developing a new program for their organization that allows for others to grow in their leadership journey. This guide can be used by governmental agencies, private business organizations, nongovernmental offices (including nonprofits), and other affiliations. It can also be used by high school and college programs to further complement core leadership curriculums. Tools within this guide could be used to help students identify their current competency levels, which can further help them to identify what they would like to do in their future careers.

This instructional guidebook is not a product of the US government, the EPA, or the US Army Corps of Engineers. The author is not doing this work in any governmental capacity. The views expressed herein are those of the author only and do not necessarily represent those of the federal government.

Finally, I recommend this guide be used and modified to meet your specific needs. Consider it a living resource.

ACKNOWLEDGMENTS

I want to provide special thanks to Angela M. Kaiser for her inspirational wisdom in encouraging me to write this manuscript and to reflect upon the concepts that I have presented herein to help my own growth.

I also want to acknowledge Craig Litteken for the technical advice and guidance he has provided through the development of this journey, which I shall always deeply appreciate.

My gratitude also goes to Barbara Chancey and many other leaders for their technical guidance and time in allowing me to bounce different ideas off them.

Finally, I want to recognize all the wonderful people at Balboa Press who have helped me to make this dream a reality.

PROGRAM BENEFITS

*Becoming a leader is the most crucial choice one can make—
it is the decision to step out of darkness into the light.*

—Deepak Chopra

Over the years and especially of late, I have met and worked with a lot of up-and-coming passionate leaders who have wanted to do great things for their organization, but limitations in their skill set prevented them from effectively implementing organizational change (or minimized their ability to do so). In most cases, they had the potential and charisma to be great leaders, but they weren't fully utilizing their strengths.

For example, their self-awareness skills were low. They were not routinely making mindful or authentic decisions, or they were not regulating their emotional intelligence. In some cases, the individual's passion was high but communication skills were ineffective. Some were being overlooked for promotions because their interview skills were weak and not on point. Additionally, there was more pressure exerted on employees to lead. This Leadership Awareness and Development Program (LADP) instructional guide provides a structured yet flexible approach that can be used year after year for nurturing and developing an individual's leadership competencies.

The purpose of this instructional guidebook is to provide the tools necessary for developing, operating, and sustaining a basic curriculum. Assessment tools will be discussed as well so that you can continually evaluate and strengthen your program. The guidebook can be used to identify future leaders' strengths so that they can more effectively use them in making decisions. Consequently, the proposed program focuses on the basic concepts of leadership and provides participants with an opportunity to learn more about their leadership skills and talents.

Specific sessions are focused on leadership, individual self-assessments, critical thinking, communications, emotional intelligence, presence (including authenticity), mindfulness, stress, conflict, negotiations, financial management and work planning, change management, program evaluation, rewards, and followership. The goal is that by the end of the program, each participant will have a self-development plan with accountability measures that will allow for each individual to further build upon personal professional competencies. In addition, individuals will understand how their leadership styles complement their organization's values, culture, mission, and vision, and how their skills can be utilized to accomplish the overall program tenets.

It is well documented in the literature that a leadership program can provide the following organizational and individual benefits:

Organizational

- increased morale, productivity, and retention
- stronger strategic vision and purpose
- a coaching/mentoring culture
- enhanced team leadership skills and a network of exceptional leaders
- stronger organizational bonds and bridges chain gaps
- enhanced ability to respond to change
- increased pool of promotable employees
- resilience that can lead to less stress and more certainty and predictability
- greater internal strengths
- positive impact on the bottom line

Individual

- a personalized approach for learning in a safe environment
  o hands-on approach with extensive coaching and feedback
  o promotes peer learning and teamwork

- boosts to morale and productivity
- a wider world of career possibilities

This instructional guide is unique and timely for the following reasons:

- There are few instructional guides in existence and none published within the last few years (that I have found) that comprehensively cover the topics addressed in the proposed guide.
- It provides practical applications and exercises for building a leadership awareness and development program plan.
- It is based on what I have learned in previous leadership development courses that I have taken throughout my twenty-five-plus-year career; what I have learned over my lifetime; what I have expected from my leaders; and insights I have gained by talking with other senior leaders inside and outside of my organization.
- It is similar to a program developed for the US Army Corps of Engineers, Savannah district, which was implemented and has been refined here based on participants' input and my personal reflection following completion of the program.
- It implements strategic and succession plans.
- It was built as a yearlong in-house course so that participants can reflect on what they've learned over the program year.
- It is based on real and direct experience, supplemented with the latest focused literature and book references to support different lesson plans and exercises—all identified in a detailed annotated agenda.
- It includes example policy and philosophy statements; example slide materials that can be used to present the program to upper management for approval; and an annotated agenda.
- It offers opportunities for coaching, peer-sharing, journaling, interviewing, briefing, facilitating, and presenting.
- It encourages participants to engage in specialized sessions on values, mission, vision, and other organizational tenets; individual and organizational competencies; blind spots; communications; emotional intelligence; workforce/work planning; and change management.

- It includes a soft and technical competency gap/needs assessment.
- It establishes a strength baseline for participants and allows an organization's specialized courses to be introduced in the program. Participants can take specialized courses based on needs identified in the basic course.
- It includes a self-development plan that can be updated annually to ensure career development that promotes individual and program needs.
- It was developed to be practicable and reasonably inexpensive to implement.

The expectation is that the course materials and mentors/coaches will help each individual build a self-development plan that will be a living document. The plan will be based on the values, mission, vision, and goals of the organization as well as the professional needs of the individual and will be reviewed and updated on an annual basis. Additionally, it is expected that all participants will be more productive than they currently are and carry more responsibilities in the organization.

This program can help to establish the foundation and set the framework for developing future organizational leaders—the best of the best—and ensure that mindful decisions move us forward together in peace and as one universally united body.

INTRODUCTION

The purpose of this instructional guidebook is to help develop future leaders as it helps them both identify their strengths and use those strengths in making decisions. The proposed program focuses on the basic concepts of leadership and provides participants with an opportunity to learn more about their leadership skills and talents. Specific sessions are focused on the following:

- leadership
- individual self-assessments
- critical thinking
- communications
- emotional intelligence
- mindfulness
- presence
- stress
- conflict resolution
- negotiation
- financial management and work planning
- program evaluation
- rewards
- followership
- change management

The goal is that by the end of the program, participants will have a self-development plan that will further build upon their professional competencies. In addition, individuals will understand how their leadership styles complement their organizations and how their skills can best be utilized to accomplish the overall program mission.

As you develop your program, check to see if your organization provides specific courses—for example, a one- or two-week course on conflict management or communication. If it does, you could ensure that an element of your program briefly introduces that topic so that the participants can get a taste of what other courses might be offered in a more in-depth course by your organization.

This book is organized into two parts, with the first part providing the framework and structure for the program and the second providing the support tools. For example, in part one, section 1 defines common terms used throughout the book; section 2 provides a program introduction and overview; section 3 provides program information; section 4 provides information on the program sessions and topics; and sections 5–10 provide information on the applicant requirements, application process, appeal process, resignation process, graduation requirements, and approval process. In part two, section 11 provides an annotated course schedule; section 12 presents a sample slide presentation; section 13 outlines book report and essay requirements; sections 14–16 provide case examples for an organizational diagnosis, competencies and self-development, and communication; section 17 provides the pretest and posttest; and section 18 provides the course assessment. There are also supplementary book references included in the different sections that could be used to further flesh out your specific lesson plan.

Note that where you see brackets, I will typically provide information to be included as text at that location or provide an example of the type of text to be filled in that location.

An Instructional Guide for
Participants, Mentors, and Supervisors

[Organization]

Leadership Awareness and
Development Program

[Date]

EXECUTIVE SUMMARY

Program Policy and Philosophy: I recommend stating in writing the organization's position on the importance of having a leadership awareness and development program. For example:

> It is important in our environment of increased retirements and constrained budgets that we continually invest in our people and develop leaders to meet the challenges of our corporate mission. This program is designed to train the rising stars of our organization as part of "building the bench." I know I can count on our leaders to fully support the Leadership Awareness and Development Program and actively engage in ensuring the right people are selected for it. There should be a continuous cycle of employees moving through the program to sustain the bench and develop the next generation of leaders.

> —[Name of director of organization, date]

This program should be housed at the highest level possible within the organization. In some cases, that may mean the CEO; in others, it's the owner. You will also need to determine which department should manage the program: planning, human resources, and so forth.

Program Focus: The proposed program is to focus on the basic concepts of leadership and provide participants with an opportunity to learn more about their leadership competencies. By the end of the program, individuals will understand how their leadership styles complement their organization and how their skills and competencies can best be utilized to accomplish the overall program mission and vision.

Group Size: The program has been designed to accommodate no fewer than ten or more than twenty employees.

Duration: This program is scheduled to occur annually, with the class starting in [May 20XX] and ending in [April 20YY].

Time Required to Complete Program: One session will be conducted monthly. Participation in the program will require approximately one hundred hours of on-duty time. Participants can expect to contribute many hours of their own time for off-duty reading, studying, and completing class assignments.

Funding: Aside from labor, training costs are estimated at approximately $[____] per participant.

Return on Investment: Return on investment will be assessed using pretest and posttest scores. Long-term assessment will compare existing competency scores against future scores.

Leadership Awareness and Development Program (LADP) Facilitator: Facilitator(s) will lead and facilitate the LADP from application to graduation and advise the LADP steering committee as necessary.

LADP Steering Committee: The steering committee is made up of senior leaders of the organization and oversees program-implementation functions.

LADP Workgroup: The workgroup consists of a subgroup of the steering committee and the supervisors. They determine course instructors as well as review and comment on proposed course materials.

Relationship to Other Organizational Leadership Programs: The proposed program provides basic knowledge and skills for developing and evaluating current staff leadership abilities. The program sessions offer an introductory level of knowledge that can provide a core foundation for more intermediate and advanced training opportunities.

Key Program Dates

No later than December 15, 20XX: Program approval

No later than February 15, 20XX: Open registration

No later than March 15, 20XX: Applications due date

No later than April 15, 20XX: Finalize class list

May 20XX: Kickoff session

March 20YY: Graduation

Graduation Requirements

- Attend *all* monthly sessions.
- Prepare monthly journal entries.
- Participate in two mentoring/coaching sessions.
- Complete self-assessment tools.
- Create or update self-development plan.
- Complete developmental opportunity.
- Read, write, and present on two leadership books.
- Write and present on personal leadership essay.
- Complete organizational diagnosis.
- Complete leadership and rubric assessment.
- Complete competency evaluation.
- Complete communication assessment.

Notes

- Participation in this program does not excuse the employee from performing the duties required by his or her assigned job.
- Participation in this program does not guarantee a promotion.

Approval Process

- [Identify approval and timing process.]

PART ONE

Program Requirements

SECTION 1

Definitions

This section defines common terms used in this document.

After-Action Reviews and Reports (AARRs): An after-action review and report is a manner in which one can discover what happened during a program or project process. The following questions should be addressed: what happened, when, where, who, and why. The review provides an opportunity to assess performance and decision-making throughout the process. It allows staff to discover program and individual competencies and to recommend process and operational improvements and ways to minimize and/or eliminate waste.

Leadership Awareness and Development Program (LADP): The LADP utilizes a framework for developing results-oriented, agile leaders with broad perspectives who lead people and lead change successfully in complex environments.

LADP candidates: Candidates are those employees who have a desire to improve their job performance and leadership skills. These are employees who have been identified by their supervisor as having potential for movement to leadership positions.

LADP course instructors: Course instructors develop course materials and present materials to participants.

1

LADP facilitator: The facilitator, an organization-designated representative or designee, will lead and facilitate the LADP from application to graduation. This member will be nominated by the LADP steering committee and confirmed by the organization's director. Ideally, the facilitator will:

- have experience in facilitating/managing leadership programs and a demonstrated desire to help participants grow as leaders;
- be selected prior to the application period for the program;
- communicate to the participants at the beginning of the program year the program expectations, the role of the LADP steering committee, the role of other leaders, and the required aspects of the program, versus those aspects of the program that are flexible;
- communicate openly with participants on issues that arise during the year, provide a forum for open dialogue on issues, and serve as a sounding board for individual participants;
- hold an informational kickoff meeting to discuss program highlights to potential organizational participants;
- consult with participants' supervisors and mentors, as needed, to maximize their involvement and contribution to participants' success and experience in the LADP;
- schedule the monthly sessions and other events, book conference rooms, and confirm speakers, as necessary;
- facilitate discussions;
- assist with monitoring and evaluating all aspects of the LADP and preparing an annual written evaluation report that contains AARRs;
- approve absence requests in coordination with the steering committee;
- brief the organization's director on a quarterly (or as-needed) basis to ensure continued understanding, support, and success of the LADP; and
- report to and advise the steering committee on status and issues.

LADP participant: A participant is an employee who applies to the program and is selected by the LADP steering committee.

LADP steering committee: The steering committee consists of senior leaders (office director, deputy directors, and division directors of the organization) and oversees program-implementation functions. More specifically, members of the committee

- perform final review and approve course curriculum;
- identify workgroup members;
- screen and review applications and conduct formal interview process, if necessary;
- narrow the candidate list, approve candidates, and approve waivers;
- notify candidates they have been chosen (or not chosen) to participate in the program;
- serve as mentors/coaches and/or approve/recommend mentors/ coaches;
- maintain contact with participants to provide advice and assistance as required;
- provide immediate and continuous feedback throughout the year to the participants and the facilitator on the execution of the program; and
- take feedback through after-action reviews and reports (AARRs) and other sources to make necessary changes and improvements to the program on an annual basis.

LADP workgroup: The workgroup consists of a subgroup of the steering committee and the supervisors. The purpose of this group is to identify and determine course instructors as well as review and comment on proposed course materials.

Leader development: Leader development is a deliberate, continuous, sequential, and progressive process—grounded in the organization's values—that develops individuals into competent and confident leaders capable of making informed decisions and taking decisive action.

Mentors and coaches: Mentors and coaches generally include those who have achieved professional success, acquired self-confidence, and experienced professional satisfaction. In turn, they wish to provide the benefit of their professional experiences to developing employees. These individuals may conduct regular sessions with LADP participants and attend the informational briefing and kickoff meeting. The mentor and/or coach and the participant will strive to develop a confidential relationship for the purpose of sharing wisdom regarding organizational culture, values, and personal/career development. The mentor and/or coach is a trusted advisor, information provider, critic, and interpreter of organizational policies and practices. They should be experienced, senior-level leaders within the organization and have demonstrated experience with mentoring or coaching. They shall be approved by the steering committee.

Supervisors: Supervisors should foster a positive and supportive attitude toward the LADP, listen to participants' concerns, provide advice and assistance to participants, and initiate discussions regarding concepts and ideas participants are learning in the LADP. Supervisors or their designated representatives may attend the informational briefing/kickoff meeting.

Each participant's supervisor will identify the most important soft and technical competencies in that individual's program. Recommend that the supervisor put together a small workgroup consisting of the most senior staff, upcoming staff, and himself or herself. Together, the workgroup will identify the top ten soft competencies and identify by rank of importance. This same drill should be completed for technical competencies too. Afterward, the workgroup should rank staff at the different competencies. Scores could be based on a number from 1 to 10, with 1 being the lowest rank and 10 the highest. Furthermore, scores could be identified as low-level competency (score between 1 and 3), midlevel competency (score between 4 and 7), and high-level competency (score between 8 and 10).

All competency ranks should be discussed with staff to ensure ranks are valid and adjusted as necessary. This exercise needs to be completed as part of session D of section 11. Recommend that all staff complete this session. The information should be used to update staff development plans.

Supervisors will identify developmental needs of their employees and discuss those needs with the participants and the facilitator for the purpose of targeted individual development planning. Supervisors will also encourage participants to apply what they learn to their day-to-day work activities and apply the learning to their own leadership activities and opportunities.

SECTION 2

Program Introduction and Overview

This section introduces the program. Among other things, it discusses intent, offers an overview, and points out the relationship to other organizational leadership programs.

A. Intent

It is our intention to have the LADP provide an opportunity for aspiring leaders to improve their leadership skills as well as tools for those graduates to further their self-continued development and growth. [The organization] fully supports this program and encourages all supervisors to promote it. Program benefits include the following:

- increased awareness of personal leadership strengths
- understanding of how effective leaders influence attitudes and behaviors
- enhanced strategic thinking, problem-solving, and negotiation skills
- ability to use collaboration and influence to drive results
- improved ability in leading teams successfully

We will have a strengthened core of skilled leaders prepared to assume greater responsibility and make increased contributions in [the organization].

B. Overview

[The organization] is seeking motivated individuals who are interested in building basic leadership skills. Individuals who participate in the LADP will learn about the traits and techniques of leaders; acquire new skills and awareness; and learn how to apply lessons learned to their career and personal life. In addition, individuals will understand how their leadership styles complement their organization and how their skills can best be utilized to accomplish the overall program mission. Program goals include the following:

- develop awareness and understanding of the visions and values of [the organization] and its leaders
- create understanding of development accountability—each person for his/her own development and each leader for his/her subordinates' development—by:
  o building individual confidence, encouraging innovation, and developing interpersonal communication skills
  o stimulating continued personal and career growth
  o strengthening leadership skills
- identify and develop a pool of potential leaders for [the organization] to draw upon in the future

This is a part-time, multifaceted program. The LADP includes an analysis of leadership style using recognized evaluation tools (including the Strengths Deployment Inventory and Myers-Briggs Type Indicator) to do the following:

- conduct a self-analysis of strengths and weaknesses
- guide preparation of a self-development plan (SDP)
- structure training sessions
- determine participation on team projects

- suggest assignments intended to broaden knowledge of leadership and management issues
- recommend [organization] meetings and other forums
- facilitate meeting discussions
- guide a mentoring relationship

Participation in the program is strictly voluntary. However, participants agree to be active members in the program and take part in all LADP activities and opportunities. Participants shall commit to actively working on self-development and building team/relationships throughout the year and supporting other participants in their development. They will be required to meet assignment deadlines. The program requires a personal investment of time for reading, preparing presentations, writing essays or brief reports, and working on projects and course work.

Individuals will participate in teams to support learning events, including classroom sessions and group events. Participants agree to give and receive open and constructive feedback and suggestions, and to maintain open channels of communication with the facilitator, instructors, and fellow participants. Continued participation in the program is subject to the participant meeting certain requirements (including class attendance and active participation in projects). Participation in this program does not excuse employees from performing the duties required by their assigned job. Neither does participation in this program guarantee a promotion.

The program agenda is provided in section 11. A program description and presentation that could be used to help sell the program is provided in section 12.

C. Relationship to Other Organizational Leadership Programs

The proposed curriculum provides basic knowledge and skills for assessing the principles of an effective leader and enhancing one's own skills. The program sessions offer an introductory level of knowledge that will provide a foundation for more intermediate- and advanced-level training opportunities. This program will be complementary with existing organizational courses, including [identify existing programs and courses]. More information is provided below for the [name of programs/courses].

[Identify and describe existing programs and courses, including purpose, focus, prerequisites, length, cost, timing, location, other relevant logistics, and where more information can be found. If there are no existing programs or courses, also note that here.]

SECTION 3

Program Information

This section provides information on the details of the program.

A. Key Program Dates

Key program dates for the first year of the program are provided in table 1.

Table 1. Key Program Dates	
Date	**Activities supporting application process and program**
NLT 15 December 20XX	Approve program.
NLT 15 February 20XX	Send email announcement to all employees in [organization] with most recent draft of the guidance manual attached.
NLT 1 March 20XX	Conduct information session on program (optional).
NLT 15 March 20XX	Conclude application process—deadline for applicants to submit signed application and required documentation to LADP facilitator.
NLT 1 April 20XX	Complete interviews, if necessary.
NLT 15 April 20XX	Finalize class list.

| May 20XX | Hold kickoff session. |
| March 20YY | Hold graduation ceremonies. |

Dates are provided as an example to project (or illustrate) scheduled activities. Dates should be set to accommodate your program needs.

B. Group Size

The program has been designed to accommodate no less than [ten] or more than [twenty] employees. More information on the application and selection process can be found in section 5.

C. Duration

The program is scheduled to occur annually, providing there are a minimum of [ten] qualified participants. The class will start in the [spring], beginning in [May of 20XX] and ending in [March of 20YY] with a graduation ceremony. Employees are expected to participate on a part-time basis while performing their assigned duties. Sessions will occur on a monthly basis.

D. Time Required to Complete Program

Participation in the program will require approximately [100 hours] of on-duty time. Participants can expect to contribute many hours of their own time for off-duty reading, studying, and completing class assignments.

E. Funding

Each participant's office will arrange funding for the labor of its participant. These funds will be considered training. Funding for personality surveys (SDI or similar) will be paid for out of [the organization's] central account. The total survey cost per participant in the program is approximately

$[_____]. [Cost can be based on different tools used in the course plus additional facilitator/instructional guide costs. Costs can be minimized where in-house organizational instructors have the appropriate skills.]

F. Return on Investment

Return on investment will be assessed using pretest and posttest scores. In addition, long-term assessments can be conducted by comparing existing competency scores against future scores. Competency reviews should occur on an annual basis.

G. Record Keeping

Record keeping shall include the following materials:

- applications
- lists of approved participants and supporting documents
- interview process notes
- course syllabi
- graduates
- lists of unapproved candidates and supporting documents

SECTION 4

Program Sessions and Topics

This section highlights program timing, topics, and dates.

There will be [11 monthly] training sessions. Participants must attend *all* sessions. It is understood that there may be times when leave, temporary duty, or other obligations make attendance impossible for participants, and in those cases, the steering committee will need to determine whether the absence is acceptable and work can be made up or if the participant should be dropped from the course.

Each session will include a leadership topic, a review of program requirements, and a chance for participants to ask any questions of the facilitator or other participants. The default dates for the [monthly] session will be the [third Thursday of each month]. This date can be changed based on holidays, mission requirements, or other conflicts. Monthly training topics and classes will be taught by invited presenters and supplemented by in-house staff.

Tentative dates and topics for the first LADP Class are provided in table 2.

Table 2. Tentative Dates and Topics	
Date	**Topic**
May 20XX	Overview
June 20XX	Self-competency assessment
July 20XX	Organizational tenets

August 20YY	Organization and technical competency assessments
September 20YY	Communications
October 20YY	Briefs and presentations
November 20YY	Conflict, stress, mindfulness, emotional intelligence, and negotiations
December 20YY	Financial management and work planning
January 20YY	Change management, program evaluation, and rewards
February 20YY	Followership and leadership reports
March 20YY	Wrap-up and graduation

Additional details on course topics are presented in section 11. Also, note that topics are tentative and may be modified each year by the steering committee.

SECTION 5

Applicant Requirements

This section discusses different characteristics and needed skills to look for in selecting potential applicants. If your needs are different from those below, you should identify what other factors you are looking for.

A. Potential Applicants

Model applicants for the LADP include [organization] employees who meet the following criteria:

- *employment status*: full-time permanent
- *years*: minimum of two years of [organization] service
- *performance*: satisfactory performance rating or above over the last two rating cycles and clearly demonstrated potential for making substantial/significant long-term contributions to [the organization]

Senior leaders (division/office directors) and members of the LADP steering committee may request a waiver of the above requirements for specific applicants. The waiver request must explain why participation in the program cannot be delayed until the applicant meets the criteria.

B. Computer Skills

Individuals should possess computer skills that will enable them to read and send email, prepare written documents, prepare presentations in PowerPoint, and complete spreadsheets in Excel.

SECTION 6

Application Process

This section outlines the application process. For example, all applicants shall complete and submit the application form provided in paragraph F by the stated deadline to be considered for the program. Applicant must meet the conditions specified in section 5 and as presented on the application. Also, it is the responsibility of the interested employee to ensure the application is received by the LADP facilitator prior to the deadline. Applications not received prior to the deadline may not be accepted unless otherwise approved by the steering committee.

Additional information follows on the nomination procedures; evaluation and selection process; equal employment opportunity; accommodations for disabled employees; documentation and record-keeping; application; and statement of understanding.

A. Nomination Procedures

Employees in the model audience who want to be considered for the program will submit the following documents, through supervisory channels, to the LADP facilitator by [15 March 20XX]: résumé and application included with this announcement (paragraph F). Interested employees are also encouraged to attend the LADP informational briefing, if offered. It is the responsibility of the interested employee to ensure the application is received by the LADP facilitator prior to the deadline.

B. Evaluation and Selection Process

The LADP facilitator will collect and evaluate applications for completeness. The facilitator will screen the applications to ensure that all sections are filled out and all signatures are obtained. The facilitator will inform applicants of whether or not they have made it past the first screening process.

Following the determination of completeness, the steering committee will convene and select the candidates to be admitted into the program. If necessary, the steering committee may decide to conduct interviews to determine final selection. Interview questions will be developed and standardized by the steering committee. Prior to the interview, the process will be explained to each candidate to be interviewed. The process will be the same for each individual candidate.

In this case, the steering committee will screen the applications and determine who will be interviewed. The committee will establish a "cut line" and determine who out of the list of candidates will be interviewed for the program. The cut line will be based on the submitted application materials and will be determined by the steering committee.

Interviews, if necessary, will be held by the dates outlined in section 3. After the steering committee selects the qualified candidates for the program, the facilitator will inform the applicants of such determinations. The overall selection goal is to have a clear list of participants established and all candidates notified of their status by [15 April], annually.

Potential interview questions include the following:

- Why are you interested in participating in the program?
- What do you see as your top three strengths and weaknesses? Provide examples.
- What steps have you taken thus far in your career to take stock of and advance your leadership skills?
- Do you have time to complete the program requirements? Explain how you will manage current work responsibilities along with program requirements.
- What are your expectations of the course?
- After completion of the program, what will be your next steps to further develop your leadership skills, and how will they be used to support organizational growth?

To score the different questions, each interviewer should assign a point value to each of the candidate responses to facilitate further discussion. Use a scale between 0 and 5—where 0 is low and 5 is high. Interviewers should discuss what the numbers would qualitatively look like for scoring purposes and then discuss scores following the interview process. If wanted, all points could be added and candidates scored based on points. The facilitator (or steering committee) should keep the records in the event that there may be an appeal so that documentation can be used to further support past decision-making and participants accepted into the program.

C. Equal Employment Opportunity

All members of the model audience will receive consideration for this developmental opportunity without regard to race, religion, color, national origin, sex, age, disability, marital status, political affiliation, or any other non-merit-related factor(s).

D. Accommodations for Disabled Employees

[The organization] will make every effort to ensure accessibility to our training programs by employees with disabilities. Please notify the LADP steering committee of any special provisions that may be necessary.

E. Documentation

Application packets will not be returned to the applicants. Participants and their mentor(s) are required to maintain documentation demonstrating the successful completion of the LADP requirements. The records will be used to verify completion of program graduation requirements.

F. Application

The following is a sample application:

Application for [Organization] LADP

1. Applicant's name:_____

2. Applicant's position in organization:_____

3. Explanation of why the applicant wants to participate in the LADP at this time:_____

_____

4. How applicant's participation will benefit the organization and its program:_____

_____

5. Start date of service with organization:_____

6. Attach most up-to-date résumé.

7. Potential coach/mentor:_____

Statement of Understanding—Applicant
I have read and understand the requirements and expectations outlined in the standard operating procedures for the LADP. I agree to complete all requirements of the program on time and to the best of my ability.

_____

Signature—Applicant   Date

Statement of Understanding—First- and Second-Line Supervisors
I have read and understand the requirements and expectations outlined in the guidance manual for the LADP. This employee has the ability to complete all of the requirements of the program. I will support and encourage this employee throughout the employee's participation in the program.

_____

Signature—First-Line Supervisor   Date

_____

Signature—Second-Line Supervisor   Date

*Application Due to LADP Facilitator [NLT 15 March 20XX]

SECTION 7

Applicant Appeal Process

This section outlines the appeal process. For example, applicants who have not been selected to participate in the program will have an opportunity to request an appeal. The request must be made in writing by the applicant within fifteen calendar days of notification that the individual was not selected for admittance into the program. The request shall identify rationale for reconsideration in writing. The steering committee will review the request and make a final decision within thirty days of receipt of said request. All decisions are final.

SECTION 8

LADP Resignation Process

This section presents the process for resigning from the program.

During the eleven-month period, a participant may resign from the program only if there are extenuating circumstances (such as family illness or increase in workload with short deadlines). Separation from [organization] will be considered an automatic resignation.

To initiate the resignation process, the participant must submit a letter to the LADP steering committee. The committee will notify the participant in writing when the resignation has been accepted.

SECTION 9

LADP Graduation Summary Requirements

This section summarizes graduation requirements, as presented in table 3 below. Specific sections are provided on attendance, journaling, developmental opportunities, self-assessment instruments, mentoring/coaching, reading assignments, personal leadership essay, organizational diagnosis, leadership and rubric assessment, competency evaluation/self-development plan, communication assessment, missed assignments/due dates, and other requirements/information.

Table 3. Graduation Requirements	
Item	**Additional Information**
Attend *all* monthly sessions, unless absence deemed acceptable by facilitator	
Monthly journal entries	Express: thoughts on what you learned personally throughout the session how the sessions relate to your profession recommended changes other thoughts on the session

Participate in two mentoring/ coaching sessions	Can be formal or informal Confirm each session by sending an email to facilitator as a record of the session
Complete self-assessments	Minimum one-page self-assessment based on inventory results and feedback from trainer, turned in to facilitator
Development opportunity	Participation in two or more of the developmental opportunities listed in paragraph C
Read, write, and present on two leadership books	*Book 1*: leadership book; minimum five-page report *Book 2*: biography of a significant leader; minimum ten-page report plus oral presentation
Write and present on personal leadership essay	Minimum three pages plus oral presentation
Organizational diagnosis	Minimum five pages plus oral presentation
Self-development plan (SDP)	Creation or update of SDP turned in to facilitator
Leadership and rubric assessment	Minimum five pages plus oral presentation
Competency evaluation	Minimum five pages plus oral presentation
Communication assessment	Completion of evaluation forms

A. Attendance

It is expected that each participant will attend *all* courses, unless the facilitator, as coordinated through the steering committee, approves the absence.

B. Journaling

Journaling can be a process of discovery. Participants should explore internal dialogue without judgment in the journal, engage in personal and deep inquiry, and notice themselves in the process of becoming the leader they aspire to be. Each participant is required to keep a journal during the course of this program to reflect on thoughts, feelings, reactions, and learning. The journal should track experiences, insights, and learning related to professional goals. Further, the journal will greatly facilitate the writing of the final paper.

For program purposes, participants should use the journal to track the following:

- learning that occurred in each class, including insights gained regarding the discipline and practice of leaders in organization and about awareness of self
- learning gained from the readings
- questions participants have about leadership and about themselves
- questions participants may want to further explore with a supervisor, mentor, or coach
- any personal issues that are showing up as a result of being in the class or that participants may be dealing with at this time
- participants' experience noticing their body as a domain of learning
- reflections, ideas, and thoughts on what makes a good leader and challenges participants encounter

The participant also shall select a journal partner from among the other participants in the program with whom the participant can discuss topics, ideas, and concerns. The participants should meet on a [monthly] basis. For example, some students may share journals with each other, some may share pages, and others may share important issues raised for them through the journaling process. Monthly summaries shall be provided to the facilitator.

C. Mentoring/Coaching

It is the rare leader, manager, or executive who has not received valuable help along the path of career development from one or more mentors/coaches. For this reason, each participant will form a mentoring/coaching relationship. Every effort will be made to establish a formal relationship between participants and the mentors/coaches of their choice.

Each participant will have the opportunity to request a specific mentor/coach during the application process. "Official" mentors/coaches may be identified by the steering committee and will serve as counselors, information providers, friendly critics, interpreters of organizational policies and practices, sounding boards, and links to the organization. Mentors/coaches should be outside of the participant's chain of command.

Mentors/coaches will be responsible for the following:

- assisting participants in developing contacts and meeting learning objectives
- devoting necessary time to work with participants
- providing regular supportive, constructive feedback (both formal and informal) to participants and their supervisors

Mentors/coaches will direct participants toward growth opportunities consistent with individual/organizational goals and validate the progress of participants.

If you are interested in learning more about mentoring and coaching, you may want to review *The Everything Coaching and Mentoring Book* by Nicholas Nigro.

D. Self-Assessment Instruments

Each participant will complete selected assessment instruments. Following these assessments, each participant may receive a one-on-one interaction with the instructor based on the findings of the inventory. Details on how this survey will be funded can be found in the "Funding" paragraph in section 3E of this guidance manual.

E. Developmental Opportunities

Participants need to choose at least two or more activities from the list below in order to complete the program. The list is subject to change. Participants should get approval from their supervisor prior to attending any of the events or opportunities to ensure that they can attend within the departmental overhead budget. Participation in these events should be coordinated through the facilitator.

Available opportunities are as follows:

- attend senior-level meetings, including budget workshops
- attend senior-leader luncheons
- shadow senior leaders
- attend public meetings
- attend [organization] offsite sessions
- attend/participate in other options as approved by facilitator

F. Reading Assignments

Participants will read a minimum of two books on leadership, with one focusing specifically on leadership styles and the other a biography on a significant leader. Participants will propose books to the facilitator and request facilitator approval prior to completing assignments.

Participants will complete a summary of the books, to include significant points, relevance, and other elements as defined by the facilitator. The first book report will be a minimum of five pages long, single-spaced, in a 12-point font. The second book report will be a minimum of ten pages long, single-spaced, in a 12-point font. Participants will also give oral presentations on their findings. See section 13.

G. Personal Leadership Essay

Participants will write a minimum of three pages on what type of leader they are. In preparing the essay, each participant shall provide a brief analysis of the different leadership styles and then discuss what style is utilized by the participant. Further, the participant shall provide case-specific examples to support the chosen leadership style. Each participant will also give an oral presentation on findings. See section 13.

H. Organizational Diagnosis

Participants will write a minimum of five pages on an analysis of the organization. In preparing the report, the participant shall provide a brief introduction on the organization and his/her role in it, as well as the following:

- branch values
- purpose
- vision
- mission
- goals and objectives
- climate and culture
- leadership style
- organizational strengths and weaknesses
- lessons learned

Each participant will also give an oral presentation on their findings. See section 14.

I. Leadership and Rubric Assessment

Participants will write a minimum of five pages on how to solve a problem identified in the organizational diagnosis. All participants will also give an oral presentation on their findings. See section 14.

J. Competency Evaluation and Self-Development Plan

Participants will prepare a personal leader-development plan to increase their understanding of themselves and their competencies as a leader. They will then devise a strategy for personal growth and achievement. Further, these strategies will be built into each participants SDP. Each participant will also give an oral presentation on these findings. See section 15.

K. Communications Assessment

Participants will complete a communication exercise that will assess how well the individual listens, understands the conversation, and provides direction. See section 16.

L. Missed Assignments/Due Dates

An important part of this program is developing self-discipline, time management, and accountability. When individuals sign up for the program, they agree to the requirements, due dates, and so forth. Participants will have to complete many of the assignments and requirements of the program after hours and on their off-duty time.

If an assignment listed above is not turned in by the due date, that participant will be sent an email with a request that the late assignment be turned in within seven days of the original due date. If the assignment is not turned in within seven days of the original due date, an email will be sent to inform the participant's supervisor of the late assignment. At that point, the supervisor can request an extension based on workload, leave, and so forth.

If the extension is agreed upon by the facilitator, the supervisor and the facilitator will agree to a new due date. If the assignment has not been turned in within thirty days of the original due date and no request for extension has been authorized, the participant will be dropped from the program and will be notified via email that he/she is no longer a candidate for graduation from the program.

M. Other Graduation Requirements/Information

- Participants are expected to maintain current workloads and existing work deadlines.
- Graduates will receive a certificate and recognition during the LADP graduation ceremony.

N. Other Requests

- Be on time.
- Silence phones, Blackberries, and the like.
- Dress business casual.
- Keep the environment safe and support each other.
- One person speaks at a time.
- Use active listening skills and encourage others to share.

SECTION 10

Approval Process

A. Program Approval

This section identifies the approval process required to gain program acceptance. There are PowerPoint presentation materials in section 12 that can be used to pitch the program to the appropriate decision-makers for approval. The presentation materials should be used to guide the discussion as well as provide a summary handout.

B. Course-Material Approval

After the program is approved, instructors are selected by the workgroup and approved by the steering committee. These instructors shall develop course materials based on the annotated agenda provided in section 11. For each course module, course material handouts shall include purpose, objectives, and a course outline with introduction, supporting materials, and conclusion.

After the course modules have been drafted, they shall be presented to the workgroup and other subject-matter experts. After final revisions have been completed for each of the course modules, the materials shall be presented to the steering committee for approval. Once approved, final materials can be prepared for participants. Following completion of the curriculum, participant and facilitator comments shall be reviewed, and recommendations may be addressed in the following year's program.

REFERENCES

Byrne, Jo-Ann C., and Richard T. Rees. *The Successful Leadership Development Program*. San Francisco: Pfiefer, 2006.

Nigro, Nicholas. *The Everything Coaching and Mentoring Book*. Avon, MA: Adams Media, 2008.

Rothwell, William J., and H. C. Kazanas. *Building In-House Leadership and Management Programs; Their Creation, Management, and Continuous Improvement*. Westport, CT: Quorum, 1999.

PART TWO

Program Support

SECTION 11

Annotated Course Schedule

This section provides an annotated course schedule that identifies program title, date, time, and location; information to guide specific activities, discussions, and exercises; and supplemental book references. For each course module, course material handouts should include purpose, objectives, and a course outline, which includes an introduction, supporting materials, and a conclusion.

A. Overview

Month [May] [Day, Date]		Conference Room
9:00–9:20	Welcome and overview	Director
9:20–10:00	Introduction ice-breaker	Facilitator
10:00–10:30	Pretest	Facilitator
10:30–10:45	Break	
10:45–11:15	Pretest discussion	Facilitator
11:15–11:30	Facilitation	Facilitator
11:30–12:30	Lunch	
12:30–1:00	Expectations and seminar administration	Facilitator
1:00–2:00	"What Is Leadership?"	Facilitator
2:00–2:15	Break	
2:15–3:15	Organizational structure	Directors/Managers

| 3:15–3:30 | Leadership homework | Facilitator |

Introduction Ice-Breaker

Allow participants to take ten minutes to get to know their neighbor. Afterward, have participants introduce the person sitting next to them by telling the class the name of the participant, the department the participant works in, why the participant is in the program, the participant's greatest work success, and what the participant would like to be doing in five years.

Pretest

Administer, grade, and discuss the test provided in section 17.

Facilitation

Discuss what facilitation is and how to lead an effective discussion. Discuss the importance of using open-ended questions.

Exercise: Participants will facilitate discussions on different leadership styles—including, for example, emotional intelligence/agility, appreciative inquiry, and leading with questions. Participants will search journal articles, request approval of a chosen article, and circulate copies to all participants at least one week prior to the session. Two participants should facilitate each article presentation and plan for a five- to seven-minute discussion (see section F, day 2).

"What Is Leadership?"

Question what a leader is and the role of a leader in the work environment. Present and discuss different leadership models, and compare and contrast leadership to management.

Webster's New Collegiate Dictionary defines *leadership* as "the capacity to guide on a way ... or direct on a course or in a direction." Leadership activities tend to be people-oriented and include leading people to promote a vision—where the department desires to be in the future. In the more traditional sense, there are essentially four different leadership approaches:

1. *Authoritarian*—The manager/leader relays instruction to employees. Generally, the manager/leader has all of the information needed to implement an activity and passes the information on to employees. This style is frequently used with a new team member learning the job.

2. *Participative*—The manager/leader maintains all authority for the final decision-making process. However, prior to decision-making, the manager/leader will discuss the approach with employees and receive input on it. This process generally affords an opportunity for employees to buy in to the process and the path forward.

3. *Delegative/Laissez-Faire*—The manager/leader provides little or no direction to employees. Authority is delegated so that employees can solve problems, make decisions, and do the work. The employees determine what needs to be done, when, and by whom. This style is generally used when employees are fully competent with the information and the task to be completed.

4. *Situational*—The manager/leader lets the situation drive the style to be used.

Additionally, leadership can be looked at from a transformational or transactional perspective. A *transformational* approach focuses on the "top line"—setting a mission and vision and then aligning processes to meet a new, desired end-state. Generally, transformational leaders use charisma, inspiration, and/or motivation to influence direction and bring about change. A *transactional* approach is focused on accomplishing day-to-day tactical activities and is based on the "bottom line." Generally, management is task-oriented, and there is an exchange of services such that rewards are provided for the effort. Typically, transactional leaders step in when employees do not meet acceptable performance and provide corrective actions (passive approach) or monitor and coach as needed (active approach) while focusing on other priorities.

Webster's New Collegiate Dictionary defines *management* as "conducting or supervising of something (as a business)." Management activities tend to be task-oriented and include day-to-day planning, budgeting, and administrative activities—those activities that drive performance and execute the mission, the primary work of the department today. In *First, Break All The Rules,* Marcus Buckingham and Curt Coffman suggest that the primary roles of a manager are to select the person, set expectations, motivate the person, and develop the person. They further discuss the primary importance of hiring based on talents needed for the position and turning them into performance rather than hiring based on knowledge and skills.

In essence, the management focus is to successfully implement the mission of the organization. For example, staff should know the organization's values, mission, and vision as well as each individual's role, responsibilities, and expectations. Managers should ensure staff have the appropriate tools to do their job; treat staff fairly and equitably; promote training opportunities as needed; and show gratitude, appreciation, and recognition for good work done.

One way to facilitate a discussion on leadership and management is to show different movie or television-show clips that use the different styles outlined above and then discuss them as a group.

Organizational Structure

Discuss the structure and functions of the organization. Senior leaders present their program mission, vision, and functions to the participants. If possible, provide a chart identifying the structural organization and a handout summarizing each of the programs.

Leadership Homework

Participants will read a minimum of two books on leadership, with one focusing specifically on leadership styles and the other a biography on a significant leader. Participants will prepare reports for each book. Reports shall summarize the significant points, relevance, and other elements as defined by the facilitator.

Participants will also give oral presentations on their findings and write an essay describing the different leadership styles and what style is utilized by the participant. Further, the participant shall provide case-specific examples to support his/her leadership style. Each participant will also give an oral presentation on his/her findings. See section 13.

Supplemental Book References

Avolio, Bruce. *Full Leadership Development.* Thousand Oaks, CA: Sage Publications, Inc., 1999.

Badaracco, Joseph L. *Managing in the Gray: 5 Timeless Questions for Resolving Your Toughest Problems at Work.* Boston: Harvard Business Review Press, 2016.

Beech, Lee Roy. *Leadership and the Art of Change.* Thousand Oaks, CA: Sage Publications, 2006.

Blanchard, Ken. *The Heart of a Leader: Insights on the Art of Influence.* Colorado Springs: David C. Cook, 2007.

Blanchard, Kenneth, PhD, Patricia Zigarmi, and Drea Zigarmi. *Leaderhip and the One Minute Manager: Increasing Effectiveness Through Situational Leadership II.* Boston: William Morrow, 2013.

Blanchard, Kenneth, PhD, and Spencer Johnson, MD. *The One Minute Manager.* New York: Berkley Books, 1982.

Blank, Warren. *The 108 Skills of Natural Born Leaders.* New York: AMACOM, 2001.

Buckingham, Marcus, and Curt Coffman. *First, Break All the Rules.* New York: Simon and Schuster, 1999.

Buckingham, Marcus, and Donald O. Clifton, PhD. *Now, Discover Your Strengths.* New York: The Free Press, 2001.

Chopra, Deepack. *The Soul of Leadership*. New York: Harmony Books, 2010.

Ciulla, Joanne B. *Ethics, the Heart of Leadership*. Westport, CT: Praeger, 2004.

Covey, Stephen R. *Principle-Centered Leadership*. New York: Simon and Schuster, 1991.

Daniels, Aubrey C. *Bringing Out the Best in People: How to Apply the Astonishing Power of Positive Reinforcement*. New York: McGraw Hill, 1999.

David, Susan, PhD. *Emotional Agility: Get Unstuck, Embrace Change, and Thrive in Work and Life*. New York: Avery, 2016.

DuBrin, Andrew J. *Leadership Research: Findings, Practice, and Skills*. New York: Houghton Mifflin, 2004.

George, Bill. *Authentic Leadership: Rediscovering the Secrets to Creating Lasting Value*. San Francisco: Jossey-Bass, 2003.

Goffee, Rob, and Gareth Jones. *Why Should Anyone Be Led by You?: What It Takes to Be an Authentic Leader*. Boston: Harvard Business Review Press, 2015.

Grimme, Don, and Sheryl Grimme. *The New Manager's Tool Kit: 21 Things You Need to Know to Hit the Ground Running*. New York: AMACOM, 2008.

Gurvis, Sandra. *Management Basics, Second Edition: A Practical Guide for Managers*. Avon, MA: Adams Business, 2008.

Hesselbein, Frances, and General Eric K. Shinseki, USA Ret. *Be-Know-Do: Leadership the Army Way*. San Francisco: Jossey-Bass, 2003.

Hyatt, Michael. *Your Best Year Ever: A 5-Step Plan for Achieving Your Most Important Goals*. Grand Rapids, MI: BakerBooks, 2018.

Kaiser, Russell L. *Practical Applications for Developing Aspiring Leaders and Managers*. In prep., 2018.

Keppen, Dave. *The Art of People: 11 Simple People Skills That Will Get You Everything You Want*. New York: Crown Business, 2016.

Marquardt, Michael J. *Leading with Questions: How Leaders Find the Right Solutions by Knowing What to Ask*. San Francisco: Jossey-Bass, 2014.

Morgenstern, Julie. *Time Management from the Inside Out*. New York: Holt, 2004.

Oakley, Ed, and Doug Krug. *Enlightened Leadership: Getting to the Heart of Change*. New York: Simon and Schuster, 1991.

Patterson, Kerry, Joseph Grenny, David Maxfield, Ron McMillan, and Al Switzler. *Influencer: The Power to Change Anything*. New York: McGraw Hill, 2008.

Rath, Tom. *StrengthsFinder 2.0*. New York: Gallup Press, 2007.

Rath, Tom, and Barry Conchie. *Strengths-Based Leadership*. New York: Gallup Press, 2008.

Smith, Hyrum W. *The 10 Natural Laws of Successful Time and Life Management: Proven Strategies for Increased Productivity and Inner Peace*. New York: Warner Books, 1994.

Tjan, Anthony. *Good People: The Only Leadership Decision that Really Matters*. New York: Portfolio Penguin, 2017.

Umlas, Judith W. *Grateful Leadership*. New York: McGraw Hill, 2013.

Webster's New Collegiate Dictionary. Springfield, MA: G. & C. Merriam Company, 1979.

Wellington, Pat. *Effective People Management.* London: KoganPage, 2011.

Whitney, Dianna, PhD, Amanda Trosten-Bloom, and Kae Rader. *Appreciative Leadership: Focus on What Works to Drive Winning Performance and Build a Thriving Organization.* New York: McGraw Hill, 2008.

Zander, Rosamund Stone. *Pathways to Possibility: Transforming Our Relationships with Ourselves, Each Other, and the World.* New York: Viking, 2016.

B. Self-Competency Assessment

Month [June] [Day, Date]		Conference Room
8:00–10:15	Johari Window model discussion	Identify instructor
10:15–10:30	Break	
10:30–12:00	Passion Survey discussion	Identify instructor
12:00–12:30	Lunch	
12:30–2:00	Gallup StrengthsFinder Survey discussion	Identify instructor
2:00–2:15	Break	
2:15–4:00	Myers-Briggs Type Indicator discussion	Identify instructor

Johari Window Model

The Johari Window model was developed by Joseph Luft and Harry Ingham in 1955. It is a great tool for identifying blind spots and improving self-awareness. The model has four quadrants:

1. Quadrant 1 (open area, upper left) represents the things you know about yourself and the things others know about you.
2. Quadrant 2 (blind area, upper right) represents the things you don't know about yourself and the things others know about you.
3. Quadrant 3 (hidden area, lower left) represents the things you know about yourself and the things others don't know about you.
4. Quadrant 4 (unknown area, lower right) represents the things you don't know about yourself and the things others don't know about you.

The ultimate goal is to enlarge the open area (quadrant 1). To enlarge this quadrant, ask for feedback and listen to what others have to share as well as share information with others. This process will promote shared discovery and self-discovery. By enlarging the open area, you can build trust with others as you share information about yourself, and with the help of feedback from others, you can learn more about yourself.

Generally, the more people know about each other, the more productive, cooperative, and effective they'll be when working together. More information is available at http://www.selfawareness.org.uk/news/understanding-the-johari-window-model. You could also try conducting a web search using "Johari Window" as the key phrase.

Passion Survey

In *Passion Styles and Career Directions*, David C. Borchard, EdD, NCC, explored the concept of brain dominance and developed an instrument to assess passion and energy use based on how people spend all (or the majority) of their time. The premise here is that where you match your passions with your career choice, you will create positive energy, and where there is not an alignment, energy will be lost or not easily recharged. Based on this analysis, one can further assess whether one is spending one's time in activities that build good or deplete good energy. More information is available at http://www.visiontrac.com/PR_Guide_Sample.pdf. You could also try conducting a web search using "Passion Styles—VisionTrac" as the key phrase.

Gallup StrengthsFinder Survey

The purpose of this assessment is to identify your strengths. Gallup's Clifton StrengthsFinder measures strength by assessing the presence of thirty-four signature "talents." Your signature talents will further help to identify your primary themes (i.e., execution, influencing, relationship building, and strategic thinking). The premise here is that after you discover your talents, you can further develop and build your primary themes.

Tom Rath and Barry Conchie in *Strengths-Based Leadership*, Marcus Buckingham and Curt Coffman in *First, Break All the Rules*, and Marcus Buckingham and Donald O. Clifton, PhD, in *Now, Discover Your Strengths* suggest that development of strengths will provide the best opportunities to enjoy personal and career success. Based on this premise, a development plan would focus on further building those talents that you excel at. That way, you can ensure your strengths complement one another.

More information on this instrument can be found at https://www.gallupstrengthscenter.com/Home/en-US/About#. You could also try conducting a web search using "Gallup StrengthsFinder" as the key phrase.

Myers-Briggs Type Indicator (MBTI)

The purpose of this assessment is to identify your primary leadership preferences—preferring or choosing one option over another. The premise of the MBTI model was based on the personality theories of Carl Jung, and this tool was developed by Katherine Briggs and Isabel Briggs Myers. This tool assesses preference based on the following questions:

- Where do you focus your energy?
- How do you gather information?
- How do you make decisions?
- How do you deal with the outer world?

If you are interested in learning more about the characteristics of the different indicators, visit http://www.myersbriggs.org/. You could also try conducting a web search using "Myers-Briggs Type Indicator" as the key phrase.

Discussion Topics

- What are your blind spots?
- What are your passions?
- What are your talents?
- What are your dominant preferences?
- Do the identifying characteristics accurately describe your traits?
- Are you comfortable with the descriptions for each instrument?
- Are you using your competencies to lead and manage work?
- What actions can you commit to taking to further develop and manage your strengths?
- How will you monitor success?

Supplemental Book References

Buckingham, Marcus, and Curt Coffman. *First, Break All the Rules.* New York: Simon and Schuster, 1999.

Buckingham, Marcus, and Donald O. Clifton, PhD. *Now, Discover Your Strengths.* New York: The Free Press, 2001.

Rath, Tom, and Barry Conchie. *Strengths-Based Leadership.* New York: Gallup Press, 2008.

Webster's New Collegiate Dictionary. Springfield, MA: G. & C. Merriam Company, 1979.

Websites and Other References

Borchard, David C., EdD, NCC. "Passion Styles and Career Directions." VisionTRAC, 2009.

Johari Window Model: http://www.selfawareness.org.uk/news/understanding-the-johari-window-model

Passion Styles and Career Directions: http://www.visiontrac.com/PR_Guide_Sample.pdf.

MyersBriggs Instrument: http://www.myersbriggs.org/.

StrengthsFinder: https://www.gallupstrengthscenter.com/Home/en-US/About#.

Strengths Deployment Inventory: http://www.developing-potential.co.uk/assets/uploads/dp05bd02f07d5e4c9ebdf2a05ffb027e67.pdf.

C. Organizational Tenets

Month [July] [Day, Date]		Conference Room
8:00–10:00	Values discussion and exercise	Identify instructor
10:00–10:15	Break	
10:15–11:30	Culture and climate discussion	Identify Instructor
11:30–12:00	Lunch	
12:00–2:00	Tenets discussion	Identify instructor
2:00–2:15	Break	
2:15–4:00	Organizational and problem assessment	Facilitator

Values Discussion and Exercise

In this session, you will define values and help participants identify their personal and organizational values.

Webster's New Collegiate Dictionary defines *values* as "something (as a principle or quality) intrinsically valuable or desirable." Values identify the interest of what you or the organization believes in and describe the core behaviors and principles that guide how a team performs in a work environment—how members will act and actions they will take. Examples of values may include being mindful, authentic, compassionate, passionate, ethical, responsible, empathetic, committed to public service.

Exercise: First, have participants identify their own personal values. In identifying values, participants should think about what is most important in their life. Where and what does each participant spend time on and why? For example, do you value reading or networking and why? What are you proud of and why? If you could interview anyone, who would it be and why? Further, assess if you are living your values. Assess whether your values are in conflict with one another. If yes, state the conflict, identify pertinent facts and assumptions, determine which is more important, and modify your values based on your decision-making process. Allow thirty minutes for this part of the exercise. Next, create small teams to identify organizational values. Have small teams present on organizational values and if they are living those values. Participants should provide examples to support their findings. Allow sixty minutes for this part of the exercise.

Culture and Climate Discussion

Culture can be defined as the shared attitudes, values, goals, and practices that characterize the larger institution. Culture guides the activities of the organization and behaviors of its members, determining what is true, right, appropriate, proper, necessary, desirable, or unthinkable. *Climate* refers to the way employees feel about their organization now. Present different examples of culture/climate surveys. Discuss the importance of the culture and climate of the organization, and identify tools to assess culture and climate.

Exercise: Have the team identify and discuss the organizational culture and climate. Allow thirty minutes for the exercise.

Tenets Discussion

Define tenets and their importance to organization. Tenets may include the following:

- *Mission*—A mission statement conveys what the organization is about, what it hopes to accomplish, whom it serves, and the values it provides to the world. An effective statement will clearly identify

47

why you are in business, guide your day-to-day decisions, and set boundaries for developing future work. This statement should define "what we do and for whom."

- *Vision*—A vision statement defines the organization's future purpose, in that it is forward-looking to what you aspire to for the organization. The vision should provide direction and outline long-term goals and objectives as well as provide inspiration and motivation for all. The vision defines and guides future work efforts. This statement should define "what we want to be and do."

- *Goals*—Goals are the broad steps that set where the program is going—what the future looks like. They should link to the vision and achieve it. Goals are broad, lofty, general, abstract, and should be results-oriented, not activity-based.

- *Objectives*—Objectives provide the "where we want to go" and the "what we want to do and when." Objectives are measureable and time-based actions to achieve the goal, so they should be clear, measurable, and concrete. Utilize SMART criteria when writing objectives:

  o **Specific**—State clearly and concisely what the goal is.

  o **Measurable**—Identify milestones for progress checkpoints and completion dates so that you know what success looks like.

  o **Attainable**—State the objective so that it is relatively achievable yet provides an opportunity for growth.

  o **Realistic**—Ensure the objective is realistic and relevant.

  o **Time-bound**—Specifically state timelines and deadlines so that it is clear when success is reached.

As previously mentioned, goals set the stage for performance, and objectives make clear where we want to go, what we want to do, and when. Objectives are measureable and time-based actions to achieve the goal. They should be clear, measurable, and concrete.

Strategies generally define how you could systematically meet an objective. Unlike objectives, strategies are general and not driven by SMART criteria. Tactics identify the specific steps for implementing a strategy. They are operational and should employ SMART criteria. Tactics are also measureable and time-based actions.

Exercise: Form small groups. Identify a company's tenets and assess how well they meet the definitions above. Each small group should discuss their findings with the larger group. Allow forty-five minutes to complete the exercise.

Organizational and Problem Assessment

The first purpose of this discussion is to identify and evaluate the driving forces of your organization. The second is to identify a significant problem in your program and utilize an analytical process to solve it. See section 14.

Supplemental Book References

Beech, Lee Roy. *Leadership and the Art of Change.* Thousand Oaks, CA: Sage Publications, 2006.

Bossiday, Larry, and Ram Charan. *Execution: The Discipline of Getting Things Done.* New York: Crown Business, 2009.

Grensing-Pophal, Lin. *The Complete Idiot's Guide to Strategic Planning.* New York: Penguin Group Inc., 2011.

Gurvis, Sandra. *Management Basics, Second Edition: A Practical Guide for Managers.* Avon, MA: Adams Business, 2008.

Kaiser, Russell L. *Practical Applications for Developing Aspiring Leaders and Managers.* In prep., 2018.

Webster's New Collegiate Dictionary. Springfield, MA: G. & C. Merriam Company, 1979.

Wellington, Pat. *Effective People Management.* London: KoganPage, 2011.

Whitney, Diana, and Amanda Trosten-Bloom. *The Power of Appreciative Inquiry: A Practical Guide to Positive Change.* San Francisco: Berret-Koehler Publishers, Inc., 2009.

D. Organization and Technical Competency Assessments

Month [August] [Day, Date]		Conference Room
8:00–10:30	Organizational and problem discussion	Facilitator
10:30–10:45	Break	
10:45–11:30	Technical competency assessment	Identify instructor
11:30–12:30	Lunch	
12:30–2:45	Technical competency assessment	Identify instructor
2:45–3:00	Break	
3:00–4:00	Self-development plan	Identify instructor

Organizational and Problem Discussion

Participants present and discuss the findings of their organizational and problem assessment. Allow ten to fifteen minutes for each participant's report to the group on his/her findings. See section 14.

Technical Competency Assessment

Webster's New Collegiate Dictionary provides the following definitions:

- *Competency*—"having a requisite or adequate ability or qualities." A competency can be a behavior or expectation that is based on knowledge, skill, or talent, and it may or may not be learned.

- *Knowledge*—"the fact or condition of knowing something with familiarity gained through experience or association." Knowledge is information that is learned.
- *Skill*—"the ability to use one's knowledge effectively and readily in execution or performance." A skill is information that is learned and employed.
- *Behavior/habit*—"the manner of conducting oneself." Like competency, behavior and habit may refer to knowledge, skill, or talent, and they may or may not be learned.
- *Talent*—"general intelligence or mental power: ability." Unlike knowledge and skill, a talent is a reoccurring pattern or prevailing attitude that is learned early in life and reinforced thereafter. Although a talent can be managed, it cannot typically be learned like a knowledge or skill late in life.

Exercise: The purpose of identifying your competencies and developing a self-development plan is to increase your understanding of the competencies needed to successfully operate under your organizational mission. See section 15.

Self-Development Plan

A self-development plan (SDP) is a living document that will allow each participant to identify existing strengths and weaknesses and identify actions to further develop and manage competencies. The SDP should outline specific actions that can be taken to promote competency growth. It should also include a monitoring plan so that the participant can ensure that growth is occurring as planned or the action can be appropriately modified. See section 15.

Supplemental Book References

Avolio, Bruce. *Full Leadership Development.* Thousand Oaks, CA: Sage Publications, Inc., 1999.

Bossiday, Larry, and Ram Charan. *Execution: The Discipline of Getting Things Done.* New York: Crown Business, 2009.

Buckingham, Marcus, and Curt Coffman. *First, Break All the Rules.* New York: Simon and Schuster, 1999.

Byrne, Jo-Ann C., and Richard T. Rees. *The Successful Leadership Development Program: How to Build It and How to Keep It Going.* San Francisco: Pfeiffer, 2006.

Kaiser, Russell L. *Practical Applications for Developing Aspiring Leaders and Managers.* In prep., 2018.

Loehr, Jim, and Tony Shwartz. *The Power of Full Engagement.* New York: The Free Press, 2003.

Rath, Tom. *StrengthsFinder 2.0.* New York: Gallup Press, 2007.

Rath, Tom, and Barry Conchie. *Strengths-Based Leadership.* New York: Gallup Press, 2008.

Webster's New Collegiate Dictionary. Springfield, MA: G. & C. Merriam Company, 1979.

E. Communications

Month [September] [Day, Date]		Conference Room
8:00–9:00	Communications discussion	Identify instructor
9:00–9:15	Break	
9:15–12:00	Communications exercise	Identify instructor
12:00–1:00	Lunch	
1:00–2:00	Communications exercise	Identify instructor
2:00–2:15	Break	
2:15–4:00	Communications exercise	Identify instructor

Month [September]	[Day, Date]	Conference Room
8:00–10:00	Communications exercise	Identify instructor
10:00–10:15	Break	
10:15–12:00	Communications exercise	Identify instructor
12:00–1:00	Lunch	
1:00–2:00	Communication exercise	Identify instructor
2:00–2:15	Break	
2:15–4:15	Strengths Deployment Inventory exercise	Identify instructor

Communications Discussion

In this session, you will define what communication is and the associated process for having effective communication. *Webster's New Collegiate Dictionary* defines *communication* as "an act or instance of transmitting ... a process by which information is exchanged between individuals through a common system of symbols, signs, or behavior." In the federal government's Office of Personnel Management (OPM) course "Executive Communications and Change" (https://leadership.opm.gov/index.aspx) and Mark Goulston's 2010 book *Just Listen*, communication is described generally as a process in which the first step is to identify the purpose of the communication, the second is to check into the other person's agenda, the third is to actively listen, the fourth is to inquire, the fifth is to summarize the discussion, the sixth is to ensure the other feels valued and concerns are addressed, and the seventh is to provide feedback.

Communications Exercise

Define what effective communication is and the associated process for having effective communication. Discuss the purpose for the conversation, the need for recognizing the other person's agenda, active listening, inquiries, summarizing the conversation, and providing feedback. To engage in critical communication, break down the communication process, practice the process, and analyze taped communications. How well do you communicate? See section 16.

Strengths Deployment Inventory Exercise

The SDI was developed by the late Elias Porter and is based on the relationship awareness theory, which stresses that motives underlie everyday behavior when we relate to one another. By looking at the motive, we can gain a clearer understanding of ourselves and of others. The SDI is now being carried out by Personal Strengths Publishing, and the instrument guides the participant to an understanding of the reasons or motives that underlie human behavior and highlights how motivation changes human behavior in conflict situations. In this way, SDI enables participants to better understand themselves and others and feel more in control of their behavioral choices, both when things are going well and during times of conflict.

Exercise: Have the instructor employ SDI and discusses individual and class findings.

Supplemental Book References

Byrne, Jo-Ann, and Richard T. Rees. *The Successful Leadership Development Program: How to Build It and How to Keep It Going.* San Francisco: Pfeiffer, 2006.

Dimitrius, Jo-Ellan, PhD, and Mark Mazzarella. *Reading People: How to Understand People and Predict Their Behavior—Anytime, Anyplace.* New York: Ballantine Books, 1999.

Fisher, Roger, and William Ury. *Getting to Yes: Negotiating Agreement without Giving In.* New York: Penguin Books, 1991.

Goulston, Mark. *Just Listen.* New York: AMACON, 2010.

Harvard Business Review. *Presentations That Persuade and Motivate.* Boston: Harvard Business School Press, 2004.

Jones, Frances Cole. *How to Wow: Proven Strategies for Presenting Your Ideas, Persuading Your Audience, Perfecting Your Image.* New York: Ballantine Books, 2008.

Kaiser, Russell L. *Practical Applications for Developing Aspiring Leaders and Managers.* In prep., 2018.

Larsen, Gail. *Transformational Speaking.* Berkeley, CA: Celestial Arts, 2009.

Nhat Hanh, Thich. *The Art of Communicating.* New York: HarperOne Publishers, 2013.

Office of Personnel Management (OPM). *Executive Communications and Change Course.* Charlottesville, Virginia. More at: https://leadership.opm.gov/index.aspx.

Patterson, Kerry, Joseph Grenny, Ron McMillan, and Al Switzler. *Crucial Confrontations.* New York: McGraw Hill, 2005.

———. *Crucial Conversations.* New York: McGraw Hill, 2002.

Solomon, Muriel. *Working with Difficult People.* New York: Prentice Hall Press, 2002.

Stoltzfus, D. Lee, PhD. *The Great Communicators II.* Glendora, CA: Royal Publishing, Inc., 1987.

Webster's New Collegiate Dictionary. Springfield, MA: G. & C. Merriam Company, 1979.

Website

Strengths Deployment Inventory: http://www.developing-potential.co.uk/
assets/uploads/dp05bd02f07d5e4c9ebdf2a05ffb027e67.pdf

F. Briefs and Presentation

Month [October] [Day, Date]		Conference Room
8:00–10:30	Business writing, briefs, and talking points	Identify instructor
10:30–10:45	Break	
10:45–11:30	Meeting management and business etiquette	Identify instructor
11:30–12:30	Lunch	
12:30–4:00	Presentation skills (video exercise)	[Organization] staff

Month [October] [Day, Date]		Conference Room
8:00–10:15	Review and critique video clips	Group
10:15–10:30	Break	
10:30–11:30	Facilitation	Group
11:30–12:30	Lunch	
12:30–2:45	Interview dos and don'ts	Panel
2:45–3:00	Break	
3:00–4:00	Interview dos and don'ts	Panel

Business Writing, Briefs, and Talking Points

First, know your audience—who are you writing to. Second, know the purpose of the communications. Be clear, concise, and simple with your message. Don't use slang. Check your tone and voice: are they appropriate for your audience? Discuss the structure of communications. For example, should the communication include sentences or talking points? Discuss how to present effective talking points and PowerPoint presentations.

Meeting Management and Business Etiquette

Discuss the following:

- importance of presence and authenticity
- how to facilitate a meeting
- how to prepare an agenda and use it to guide the meeting discussion
- appropriateness of supporting tools, such as PowerPoints

Presentation Skills (Video Exercise)

Imagine you were recently promoted to be the new CEO of your organization and are expected to address your employees in a town hall meeting. You expect approximately five hundred employees to listen to your motivational speech. You have approximately five minutes to share your mission, vision, and how you will lead change. Note that the company has recently downsized and morale is at an all-time low; it will be a tough crowd, and you can expect hard questions. Additionally, you will videotape your presentation, and taped videos will be critiqued by class participants, with feedback indicators including presence, engagement, and message.

Facilitation

Conduct leadership discussions to be facilitated by two-person teams presenting on leadership styles—including, for example, emotional intelligence, appreciative inquiry, and other journal articles. Participants will facilitate the discussions. Schedule five to seven minutes for each facilitated discussion. Feedback indicators to observe include use of open-ended questions, presence, and engagement.

Interview Dos and Don'ts

Discuss how to prepare for an interview and the dos and don'ts of the interview as well as the importance of presence. Allow fifteen minutes for discussion. Each participant shall interview for the next higher position in his/her career profession. A panel should include four participants. Questions could include the following:

- What attracted you to apply for this position?
- What are your top three strengths and three weaknesses? Provide supporting rationale.
- How do you manage a heavy workload, set priorities, complete tasks in a timely manner, and handle the pressure of deadlines? Provide at least one example.
- How do you negotiate or resolve major conflicts with a supervisor and/or a difficult customer? Provide examples demonstrating your approach for resolution and discuss the success of your approach and what you learned.
- If your management was about to implement a policy you disagreed with, how would you handle it? If you have been in this position before, identify what actions you took and the outcomes of your approach. What did you learn from this experience?
- Work in the program can be very intense and time-consuming because of the high visibility and politicized nature of our issue areas. How do you personally try to keep a balance between work and non-work, and what would you do to encourage or help team members achieve a balance as well?
- How do you "manage up," including your approach for responding to upper-management requests?
- Describe what you feel are the immediate needs and opportunities of the program. What actions would you take to advance them?
- Please tell us why you are interested in this position and how you believe your qualifications make you the best candidate. Also, explain how the work in this position will advance your long-term career goals.
- Do you have any questions for the panel?

After conducting the interview, critique it, using questions like the following:

- Is the interviewee's response clear, concise, and responsive to the question?
- Is the response supported with examples?
- Is the interviewee fully engaged and present in the process?
- Does the interviewee greet and thank the panel?
- What type of body language is used during the interview, and does it reinforce the response?
- Does the interviewee summarize why he/she is best for the job?
- Does the interviewee back up statements with examples?
- Does the interviewee ask questions of the panel?
- Does the interviewee dress appropriately for the position?
- Is the interviewee authentic?
- Is the interviewee a good fit for the organization?

G. Conflict, Stress, Mindfulness, Emotional Intelligence, and Negotiations

Month [November] [Day, Date]		Conference Room
8:00–10:30	Conflict, stress, mindfulness, and emotional intelligence	Identify instructor
10:30–10:45	Break	
10:45–12:00	Negotiations	Identify instructor
12:00–1:00	Lunch	
1:00–4:00	Negotiations	Identify instructor

Conflict

Discuss what conflict is; whether it is positive or negative; and how it can be managed to promote new opportunities. *Webster's New Collegiate Dictionary* defines *conflict* as a "mental struggle resulting from incompatible or opposing needs, drives, wishes, or external or internal demands." Thus, a conflict can occur when one perceives that there is a threat to one's needs, interests, and/or concerns. Are they predictable? What triggers conflict in the work environment? What is the general response and results? How can you better manage conflict? What actions are you willing to take? Also, if the participants completed the SDI, I recommend you revisit and discuss their conflict sequence.

Stress

Discuss what stress is, what the triggers and signs are, and different ways of minimizing or reducing stress. *Webster's New Collegiate Dictionary* defines *stress* as "a physical, chemical, or emotional factor that causes bodily or mental tension and may be a factor in disease causation." Stress is a perception that creates discomfort—such as feeling pressure, feeling like you are out of control, or feeling like you are in danger. Stress can be a motivator when it occurs over a short period and in short doses, and it can result in cognitive and physical performance benefits.

Stress can also result in a variety of physical, emotional, and behavioral responses. For example, symptoms of physical stress include muscle tension; cold, clammy skin; dry mouth; headaches; fatigue; restlessness; sleep disorders; and high blood pressure. Signs of emotional stress include irritability, anxiety, anger, and/or depression. Behavioral stress indicators include watching excessive amounts of TV, spending excessive time playing computer games, drinking excessive amounts of alcohol, and/or lacking focus.

What causes stress? It happens when we perceive that something is going to occur that we may not be able to control or understand the consequences. Generally, this type of stress occurs when you perceive a negative response to an action to be taken or one that has been taken. For example, stress could occur if your values, passions, and talents don't align. What factors are creating stress in your work and home life? Work stress could be caused by a new job, new supervisor, new project, and so on. Home stress could be caused by moving, relationship problems, or financial issues.

Exercise: Are there factors that are causing stress in your life today?

For awareness purposes, take some time and create a list of the different stressors in your life. If you are looking for additional sources and different types of stress tests, you can search the internet using the keywords "stress" or "stress tests." After you determine your primary stressors, ask why and identify the underlying fear or perception. As you are working through the negative stress, try to rewrite that story into a positive one or see the gift in what is happening, if you can. Can you manage the stress? What positive actions can you take? Write them down, post them where they are visible to you, and act on them. If you are hitting obstacles that you cannot overcome, you may want to seek professional help.

Mindfulness

Discuss what mindfulness is and different ways of ensuring mindfulness. *Webster's New Collegiate Dictionary* defines *mindfulness* as "being aware" and living in the "here and now." Being mindful is being self-aware and situationally aware of your environment and acknowledging and accepting what is occurring—in other words, being present in the moment with your focus on the here and now while realizing that we are all connected within the universe. If you are unsure of how to get into your comfort zone, stop and breathe. Take several deep breaths and let everything go.

Do you think stress levels could be lower if people were more mindful? Mindfulness allows us to monitor our stress levels so that actions can be appropriately taken, like pausing and breathing. These actions will help us to get into the here and now and allow for the heart rate to slow and blood pressure to fall. Deep breathing provides more oxygen to your body and helps to relax muscles, which releases tension. Pausing and breathing further allow you to let go of difficult thoughts and emotions so that you don't get stuck.

Anna Black indicated in *Mindfulness Work* (2014) that the following have been reported as benefits of learning and employing mindfulness and mindfulness meditation:

- more energy, less anxiety, and more stability
- improved ability to manage stress and well-being

- improved ability to focus
- improved ability to actively listen and make decisions
- increased engagement in work

Note that the above summary is only a partial list. The full list is identified in the book *Mindfulness Work.*

Some tricks that help me manage conflict and stress are to manage my time, plan priorities, break big jobs down into smaller pieces, and use lots of positivity and laughter. For example, I try to be fully engaged in discussions so that I understand the expectations and can possibly shape the outcomes. In discussions, I am open and honest, and I look for the win-win by assessing options based on the intrinsic values. Further, as I am a morning person, I schedule my most important work for that time period. I also try to take breaks at least every sixty to ninety minutes—even if only to get some water or use the restroom. I may also take some deep breaths and stretch to ground myself. I also take a few weeks off a year—plan those vacations—to help keep life fresh. What can you do, and what actions can you commit to taking?

Emotional Intelligence

Discuss what emotional intelligence is. Dr. David Walton, in *Emotional Intelligence: A Practical Guide*, generally defines emotional intelligence as the ability to successfully manage yourself and the demands that you are working under. Are you aware of how your emotions affect your behaviors? What triggers a fight-or-flight response? How do and can you manage your emotions? Are you perceptive of others' emotions and behaviors? How do you manage those?

Note that if you have little experience in this field, you may want to review *Emotional Intelligence: A Practical Guide.* I also recommend that as an exercise, you consider employing a web-based instrument so that participants can explore their emotional intelligence levels and discuss their findings.

Negotiations

Discuss the practice of negotiating and how to have an effective negotiation. For example, while at the Leadership for a Democratic Society, I took a negotiations course led by William Lincoln—a very well-known national and international negotiator. (His résumé can be viewed at the website of the Lincoln Institute (http://www.thelincolninstitute.cc/about/our-people/). In the course, he broke down the art of negotiation as a process where you should identify the following elements to help guide your negotiation:

- your intangible interests
- all potential issues
- consequences of no action, an impasse, or prolonged dispute
- realistic alternatives to settlement
- your current predetermined final offer
- your fallback option
- your preferred settlement
- your secondary option
- your tertiary (or subsequent) option

Exercise: The goal in a negotiation is to work out a reasonable and equitable deal. Divide the group into two teams and give them the following information:

- *Team 1:* You and your team members are part of the union, and your team is requesting higher wages. Background: nonmanagers have not received raises within the last three years. Staff members believe productivity and sales are at an all-time high for the organization.
- *Team 2:* You and your team members are part of management, and you have to inform the union that productivity and sales are at an all-time low for the organization. Background: managers have not received raises within the last three years.

63

Did you identify the intrinsic values at risk? Did you reach a common understanding and an acceptable path forward for both parties? Why or why not?

Supplemental Book References

Bailey, Chris. *Accomplishing More by Managing Your Time, Attention, and Energy: The Productivity Project.* New York: Crown Business, 2016.

Black, Anna. *Mindfulness at Work: Reduce Stress, Live in the Moment, and Be Happier and More Productive at Work.* New York: CICO Books, 2014.

Booher, Dianna. *Creating Personal Presence: Look, Talk, Think, and Act Like a Leader.* San Francisco: Berrett Koehler Publishers, Inc., 2011.

Fisher, Roger, and William Ury. *Getting to Yes: Negotiating Agreement Without Giving In.* New York: Penguin Books, 1991.

Fredrickson, Barbara L., PhD. *Positivity.* New York: MJF Books Fine Communications, 2009.

Goldsmith, Marshall, and Mark Reiter. *What Got You Here Won't Get You There.* New York: Hachette Books, 2007.

Goleman, Daniel. *Emotional Intelligence: Why It Can Matter More Than IQ.* New York: Bantam Books, 2005.

Harris, Sam. *Waking Up: A Guide to Spirituality Without Religion.* New York: Simon and Schuster Paperbacks, 2014.

Kaiser, Russell L. *Practical Applications for Developing Aspiring Leaders and Managers.* In prep., 2018.

Lehr, Jim, and Tony Schwartz. *The Power of Full Engagement: Managing Energy, Not Time, Is the Key to High Performance and Personal Renewal.* New York: The Free Press, 2002.

Mckenzie, Stephen, Dr., *Mindfulness at Work: How to Avoid Stress, Achieve More, and Enjoy Life!* Pompton Plains, NJ: Career Press, 2015.

Patterson, Kerry, Joseph Grenny, Ron McMillan, and Al Switzler. *Crucial Confrontations.* New York: McGraw Hill, 2005.

———. *Crucial Conversations.* New York: McGraw Hill, 2002.

Walton, David, Dr. *Emotional Intelligence: A Practical Guide.* New York: MJF Books Fine Communications, 2012.

Webster's New Collegiate Dictionary. Springfield, MA: G. & C. Merriam Company, 1979.

Williams, Mark, and Danny Penman. *Mindfulness An Eight-Week Plan for Finding Peace in a Frantic World.* New York: Rodale, 2012.

Zander, Rosamund Stone. *Pathways to Possibility Transforming Our Relationships with Ourselves, Each Other, and the World.* New York: Viking, 2016.

H. Financial Management and Work Planning

Month [December] [Day, Date]		Conference Room
8:00–10:00	Work planning	Identify instructor
10:00–10:15	Break	
10:15–12:00	Work prioritization	Identify instructor
12:00–12:30	Lunch	
12:30–2:00	Financial management	Identify instructor
2:00–2:15	Break	
2:15–4:00	After-action reviews and reports	Identify instructor

Work Planning

To initiate the work-planning process, first do the following:

- Review/adjust mission, vision, goals, objectives, and the like.
- Review last year's work plan:
  o elements and assumptions,
  o what work was completed and by whom,
  o what work needs to be carried forward and by whom, and
  o what dollars were spent and what needs to be carried forward.
- Identify all new assumptions that could affect the development of your budget.
- Identify known factors that could affect the development of your budget.
- Identify workforce competencies and needs.
- Identify and understand performers (e.g., partners and stakeholders) and influencers (e.g., customers, competitors, and others).
- Identify potential projects and project-related costs.
- Identify potential budget—monies to be applied for in-house costs and contract support.

Work Prioritization

To initiate the prioritization phase, do the following:

- Identify work prioritization criteria.
- Apply factors to different projects (e.g., does it fit the mission/vision, is it discretionary, risks of not doing the project, business rationale for moving forward with it).
- Identify benefits and costs.
- Assess project alignment/schedules along with staff/contract support, budget, and benefits/costs.
- Identify preferred plan.

Financial Management

To implement your approved plan, do the following:

- Discuss plan with staff and contractors and make expectations known.
- Identify monitoring (e.g., lead and/or lag) factors and implementation strategy.

After-Action Reviews and Reports (AARRs)

The review should typically include at a minimum the following elements:

- background information (team members, roles, etc.)
- project description and purpose
- description of what happened and whether everything went as planned and detailed
- issues raised during the process and path forward
- what went right and what didn't
- any perceived benefits
- whether the project will be done again, if applicable
- lessons learned or recommendations, including current method and rationale
- what can be built upon and transferred to other projects
- ways to cut waste and increase productivity in future operations

Supplemental Book References

Hesselbein, Frances, and General Eric K. Shinseki, USA Ret. *Be-Know-Do: Leadership the Army Way.* San Francisco: Jossey-Bass, 2003.

Kaiser, Russell L. *Practical Applications for Developing Aspiring Leaders and Managers.* In prep., 2018.

Price, Mark, Walter Mores, and Hundley M. Elliotte. *Building High-Performance Government Through Lean Six Sigma.* New York: McGraw Hill, 2011.

I. Change Management, Program Evaluation, and Rewards

Month [January] [Day, Date]		Conference Room
8:00–10:30	Change management	Identify instructor
10:30–10:45	Break	
10:45–12:00	Program evaluation	Identify instructor
12:00–1:00	Lunch	
1:00–2:00	Program evaluation	Identify instructor
2:00–2:15	Break	
2:15–4:00	Rewards	Identify instructor

Change Management

Define what change management is and the associated process for making change. In discussing change management, focus on the following steps:

1. Preparing for change
2. Developing a change management plan
3. Communicating the plan
4. Implementing the plan
5. Assessing plan implementation

Remember, common factors to address in leading change are audience fear (real or perceived), what's in it for them, and who will gain/lose power.

Exercise: Employ the change style indicator instrument, as described in the *Change Style Indicator* from Discovery Learning International. The book explores the relationship of change and change management, leading to the development of a change preference and a change style indicator, such as conserver, pragmatist, or originator. The instrument allows users to identify how they faces change and how to work with others when leading, supporting, or collaborating. It also provides recommendations on how to ensure the greatest degree of flexibility and effectiveness. More information is available at http://www.discoverylearning.com.

Program Evaluation

Discuss the importance of reviewing program elements in order to cut waste and improve efficiencies. Program evaluation tools include the following:

- Just Do It
- process walk
- 5S (sort, straighten, shine, standardize, and sustain)
- visual controls
- value-stream mapping
- Kaizen event
- Lean Six Sigma

Exercise: Establish small teams (or one large team) and have them map out in-office mail-delivery processes. Identify all steps and do-loops. Discuss the overall process and determine if redundancy or duplication occurs and is necessary. If waste is identified, modify the process to eliminate it. Ideally, over time, you would want to assess the success of any modifications. You may determine additional opportunities to eliminate waste and increase productivity.

Rewards

Discuss the importance of gratitude and rewards.

Supplemental Book References

Baker, Dan, PhD, and Cameron Stauth. *What Happy People Know.* Emmaus, PA: Rodale, 2003.

Collins, Jim. *Good to Great.* New York: Collins, 2001.

Daniels, Aubrey C. *Bringing Out the Best in People.* New York: McGraw Hill, 2000.

Fredrickson, Barbara L. PhD. *Positivity.* New York: MJF Books, 2009.

Kaiser, Russell L. *Practical Applications for Developing Aspiring Leaders and Managers.* In prep., 2018.

Kellar, Gary, and Jay Papasan. *The One Thing: The Surprisingly Simple Truth Behind Extraordinary Results.* Austin, TX: Bard Press, 2012.

McFarland, Keith R. *The Breakthrough Company.* New York: Crown Business, 2008.

Price, Mark, Walter Mores, and Hundley M. Elliotte. *Building High-Performance Government Through Lean Six Sigma.* New York: McGraw Hill, 2011.

Umlas, Judith W. *Grateful Leadership.* New York: McGraw Hill, 2013.

Zaffron, Steve, and Dave Logan. *The Three Laws of Performance: Rewriting the Future of Your Organization and Your Life.* San Francisco: Jossey-Bass, 2009.

J. Followership and Leadership Reports

Month [February] [Day, Date]		**Conference Room**
8:00–10:00	Followership	Identify instructor
10:00–10:15	Break	

10:15–12:00	Present and discuss book reports/SDPs	Group discussion
12:00–12:30	Lunch	
12:30–2:00	Present and discuss book reports/SDPs	Group discussion
2:00–2:15	Break	
2:15–2:00	Present and discuss book reports/SDPs	Group discussion

Followership

Discuss what followership is and the different stages of being a follower. Ira Chaleff, in *The Courageous Follower*, identified four primary types of followers, including the partner (high support, high challenge); implementer (high support, low challenge); individualist (low support, high challenge); and resource (low support, low challenge). Note that if you have little experience in this field, you may want to review some of Ira Chaleff's works, including *The Courageous Follower*. I hope you will find it as enlightening as I did. I recommend reinforcing followership principles using video vignettes and survey participants to identify what kind of follower individuals believe they are and why.

Leadership Book Reports and Essay Requirements

See section 13.

Supplemental Book References

Chaleff, Ira. *The Courageous Follower.* San Francisco: Berrett-Koehler Publishers Inc., 2009.

George, Michael L., David Rowlands, Mark Price, and John Maxey. *The Lean Six Sigma Pocket Toolbook.* New York: McGraw-Hill, 2005.

Price, Mark, Walter Mores, and Hundley M. Elliotte. *Building High-Performance Government Through Lean Six Sigma*. New York: McGraw Hill, 2011.

K. Wrap-Up and Graduation

Month [March] Day [No., Thursday], Year [20__]		Conference Room
9:00–10:00	End-of-course survey	Facilitator
10:00–11:00	Posttest and course assessment	Facilitator
11:00–1:00	Lunch	
1:00–3:00	Graduation	Director of organization

Posttest

Administer, grade, and discuss test provided in section 17.

Program Course Assessment

See section 18.

SECTION 12

Sample Presentation-Material Messages

This section includes messaging for developing a PowerPoint presentation. These materials should be used to help gain the necessary approvals in your organization. Use the presentation materials to "sell" the program to upper-level management for approval purposes. If you need to modify it to stress a specific need in your organization, do it. However, don't reinvent the wheel if you don't have to.

For example, if you have a series of presentations that you may need to give to different senior leaders, make sure that you listen to their feedback so that you can modify the presentation to meet your needs as you go through the approval chain. Also, you may want to break the presentation up into two sessions, with the first session discussing the below materials and the second session discussing the agenda topic items to cover during the course.

Slide 1: Title Page

Organization Name

Leadership Awareness and Development Program (LADP) Proposal   [Date]

Slide 2: Need for Program

- low morale
- no/limited monetary awards for performance
- limited hiring and promotion opportunities
- need for staff to gain broad-based leadership skills

Slide 3: LADP Summary

- purpose
- outline
- key dates
- graduation requirements
- next steps
- final thoughts

Slide 4: Purpose

- The proposed program will focus on the basic concepts of leadership and provide participants with an opportunity to learn more about their leadership skills and styles.
- Specific sessions will be developed to focus on leadership, individual self-assessments, communications, conflict resolution, negotiation, financial management and work planning, followership, and change-management skills.
- Individuals will understand how their leadership styles complement their organization and how their skills can best be utilized to accomplish the overall program mission and vision.

Slide 5: Program Outline

- **Group size:** The program has been designed to accommodate no less than ten or more than twenty employees.
- **Duration:** This program is scheduled to occur annually. The class will start in May 20XX. One session will be conducted on a monthly basis over an eleven-month period.
- **Time required to complete program:** Participation in the program will require approximately 100 hours of on-duty time. Participants can expect to contribute many hours of their own time for off-duty reading, studying, and completing class assignments.
- **Funding:** Aside from labor, extramural training costs are estimated at approximately $_____ per participant.
- **Return on investment:** Return on investment will be assessed using pretest and posttest scores. Long-term assessment will compare existing competency scores against future scores.

Slide 6: Program Outline

- **LADP facilitator:** The facilitator will lead and facilitate the LADP from application to graduation.
- **LADP steering committee:** The LADP steering committee chairperson is _____ of the senior leader team. Committee representatives include _____ and the LADP facilitator.

- **Relationship to other organizational leadership programs:**
  - o This course provides basic knowledge and skills for developing and assessing leadership goals.
  - o The program sessions will offer an introductory level of knowledge to provide a foundation for more intermediate- and advanced-level training opportunities.

Slide 7: Key Program Dates

- NLT 15 DEC 20XX: Program approval
- NLT 15 FEB 20XX: Open registration
- NLT 15 MAR 20XX: Application due date
- NLT 15 APR 20XX: Finalize class list
- MAY 20XX: Kickoff session
- MAR 20YY: Graduation

Slide 8: Graduation Requirements

- Attend *all* monthly sessions.
- Prepare monthly journal entries.
- Participate in two mentoring/coaching sessions.
- Complete self-assessment tools.
- Create or update self-development plan.
- Complete developmental opportunity.
- Read, write, and present on two leadership books.
- Write and present on personal leadership essay.
- Complete organizational diagnosis.
- Complete leadership and rubric assessment.
- Complete competency evaluation.
- Complete communication assessment.

Slide 9: Agenda

A. Overview
B. Self-competency assessment
C. Organizational tenets
D. Organizational and technical competency assessments
E. Communications
F. Briefs and presentations
G. Conflict, stress, mindfulness, emotional intelligence, and negotiations
H. Financial management and work planning
I. Change management, program evaluation, and rewards
J. Followership and leadership reports
K. Wrap-up and graduation

Slide 10: Next Steps

- Share conceptual plan with other midlevel managers and revise plan as appropriate.
- Request concurrence to move forward with LADP proposal (November).
- Brief management council (November–December).
- Update draft LADP plan.
- Develop communication strategy.
- Proposed start date is May.

Slide 11: Final Thoughts

- Participation in this program does not excuse employees from performing the duties required by their assigned jobs.
- Participation in this program does not guarantee a promotion.

SECTION 13

Leadership Book Reports and Essay Requirements

This section provides more information on required book reports and essays. Participants will read a minimum of two books on leadership, with one focusing specifically on leadership styles and the other a biography on a significant leader. Participants will prepare reports for each book. They will also write an essay describing the different leadership styles and what style they personally utilize. Further, participants shall provide case-specific examples to support their leadership style. Participants will also give oral presentations on their findings. The following are requirements for each task.

A. Book Report #1: Leadership Styles

The report should include the following:

- title
- background
- reason for choosing this book
- key leadership style/characteristics discussed
- relationship to participant's individual style—where is it similar or different
- relevance in today's environment—why or why not

The report shall be a minimum of five pages in length, single-spaced, in a 12-point font. For assessment purposes, ask, "Does the report clearly discuss the above topics?" If not, discuss which topics could be strengthened and how.

B. Book Report #2: Biography of a Significant Leader

The report should include the following:

- title
- background
- reason for choosing this leader
- key leadership style/characteristics
- subject's style change over time—why or why not
- relevance in today's environment—why or why not

The report shall be a minimum of ten pages in length, single-spaced, in a 12-point font. For assessment purposes, ask, "Does the report clearly discuss the above topics?" If not, what topics could be strengthened and how?

C. Essay: Personal Leadership Style

The essay should include the following:

- What type of leader are you currently and why?
- How would you describe your leadership style? Please provide specific examples with a project, initiative/effort, or team where you demonstrated your skills, knowledge, and leadership attributes and capabilities.
- What are those attributes/traits that make you an exceptional leader?
- What are some key characteristics/attributes/traits that are essential to being a great leader? Which ones do you possess? Which ones do you want to develop further? Why do you believe these are critical?
- How do you influence others? Do you believe that you are successful in the way you influence other stakeholders, team members, and

leaders? What have you noticed in the way that you influence others? Is it positive? Are there negative or detrimental impacts (to you, the team, the organization)?

- What type of leader would you like to develop into in the future and why?

The essay shall be a minimum of three pages in length, single-spaced, in a 12-point font. For assessment purposes, ask, "Does the report clearly discuss the above topics?" If not, what topics could be strengthened and how?

D. Presentation

Participants will blend the two book reports and essay into one presentation that includes the following:

- discussion of the leadership styles presented in the books
- discussion of the essay questions above and how they relate to your leadership style
- examples to support your statements

Presentation length should be approximately fifteen to thirty minutes. Presenters should be prepared to address participant questions. Feedback considerations are as follows:

- How well does the participant address the report and presentation questions above and why/why not?
- Are there any recommendations?
- Are the organizational values clearly articulated and described with observable behaviors?
- Are the following presented and analyzed: purpose, vision, mission, climate, and culture of the organization?
- Are the goals clear and objectives SMART?
- Are strengths, weaknesses, opportunities, and threats clearly identified?
- Does the presentation include lessons learned?

SECTION 14

Organizational Diagnosis and Problem Assessment

This section discusses the requirements and outlines the steps for completing an organizational diagnosis and problem assessment.

A. Organizational Diagnosis

The purpose of this exercise is to identify and evaluate the driving forces of your organization. Each participant shall do the following:

1. Present functions of the organization.
2. Define organizational values.
3. Identify the organization's purpose.
4. Define mission statement:
   - analysis
   - revised mission
5. Define vision statement:
   - analysis
   - revised vision
6. Identify goals and objectives.
7. Discuss climate and culture:
   - climate
   - culture

8. Present organizational strengths and weaknesses.
9. Present opportunities and threats.
10. Questions for consideration:
    - Are the values congruent with the mission and vision?
    - Do the goals and objectives support the mission and vision?
    - Are the goals identified as broad steps that direct where the program is going?
    - Are the objectives SMART (specific, measurable, achievable, realistic, and time-related)?
    - Do the climate and culture reflect the values?
    - What is working well?
    - What is not working well?
11. Lessons learned

Feedback Considerations

- Are the organizational values clearly articulated and described with observable behaviors?
- Are the following presented and analyzed: purpose, vision, mission, climate, and culture of organization?
- Are the goals clear and objectives SMART?
- Are strengths, weaknesses, opportunities, and threats clearly identified?
- Are lessons learned presented?

B. Organizational Problem Assessment

This second element of the organizational diagnosis assessment requires you to apply an analytical process to solve a significant problem in your program. *Note:* You must get approval from the facilitator for your problem prior to beginning this element.

Requirement

Select a significant problem that you identified in the organizational diagnosis. Provide some background and context for your problem, addressing its significance to your program. In other words, how would this problem, left unsolved, impede mission accomplishment and organizational efficiency?

Apply the following problem-solving model to your problem. Use the following paragraph headers to clearly identify each step of the model and use narrative format to clearly explain what you did at each step:

- Identify and define the magnitude of the problem.
- Gather information.
- Brainstorm possible solutions to the problem.
- Define criteria for evaluation.
- Analyze possible solutions:
  - Present data in a matrix for comparison purposes.
  - Metrics may include practicability, feasibility, cost, legality, rightness for today, rightness for tomorrow, whether we can we live with it, and so on.
- Select the best solution.
- Identify what success looks like.
- Propose contingency measures.
- Define monitoring program.

For the analysis, identify and analyze at least three different alternatives to solve your problem.

Feedback Considerations

- Is the problem and are the consequences clearly stated and addressed?
- Is the problem-solving model properly implemented?
- Are three or more alternatives identified and evaluated?
- Are the same criteria used to evaluate each alternative?
- Does the rationale support the recommended path forward and identify what success looks like along with contingency and monitoring provisions?

SECTION 15

Competencies and Self-Development Plan

This section defines how to complete a competency evaluation and a self-development plan. After the competency exercise has been completed, be sure to review the feedback so that you can determine if there are recommended changes that may make for a stronger program the following year. For the self-development plan, ensure that participants use the form to best support their learning goals and objectives.

A. Competency Evaluation

The purpose of this exercise is to increase your understanding of your competencies. You will also prepare a plan that will allow you to further develop those competencies. In your plan, you will outline your goal and identify objectives in specific and measureable terms. The development plan requires you to pull everything together; synthesize the information; evaluate your strengths, weaknesses, and performance; and continue to plan your development as a leader.

Requirements

Identify and define *two* leadership competencies that you would like to develop when you return to your office. In determining which competencies to strengthen, you may want to identify the following:

- the goal or goals
- what's getting in the way of accomplishing the goal
- competing commitments and assumptions
- actions to be taken and a timeline for those actions

The competency goal for this exercise should include actions that would require you to close the gaps between the leader you are now and the leader you would like to become in the future. First, identify and rank the ten most important competencies used in your part of the organization. Next, identify your strength at each of the different competencies. You may want to rank your strengths based on a scale with a low of 1 and a high of 10. Next, you will need to determine which two competencies you want to improve upon. Addressing each competency separately, discuss the following:

- why the competency is important to you and how it aligns with organizational competencies
- others who will be affected and why
- specific steps you will take to reach your goal, including a timeline for implementation
- resources you will need and how you will get and use them
- personal and environmental obstacles that may prevent you from achieving your goal
- how you will measure your success
- what you have learned and how you will apply it within your organizational unit

Develop an assessment form to ensure the project purpose is met. You will also want to record your findings in your self-development plan.

Feedback Considerations

- Are the organizational as well as your individual competencies clearly stated and ranked with rationale justifying ranks?
- Are the importance and consequences of strengthening selected competencies clearly explained?
- Does the plan identify what success is, what target deadlines are, and what contingencies and monitoring may include?
- Are lessons learned discussed?

B. Self-Development Plan

An SDP is a plan that will allow each participant to identify existing strengths and weaknesses, as well as actions to further develop and manage competencies. The plan should outline specific actions that can be taken to promote competency growth. The plan should also include a monitoring component so that the participant can ensure that growth is occurring as planned or the action can be appropriately modified. This plan should be reviewed and updated as a living document, as it can be one of the most important tools in shaping your leadership journey.

Organization:_____
Program:_____
Position:_____
Leadership_____
    Type:_____
    Position:_____
Mission:_____
Vision:_____
Core values:_____
Knowledge:_____
Skills:_____
Passion styles:_____
Energy drivers:_____
Energy users:_____
SDI preference:_____
MBTI preference:_____

Gallup StrengthsFinder Survey Results

Talent strengths: Talent management opportunities:

1. _____   1. _____
2. _____   2. _____
3. _____   3. _____
4. _____   4. _____
5. _____   5. _____

Behavior strengths: Behavior opportunities:

1. _____   1. _____
2. _____   2. _____
3. _____   3. _____
4. _____   4. _____
5. _____   5. _____

Comments:

Leadership feedback themes:

     Strengths:_____

     Management opportunities:_____

Past soft development activities and courses:

1. _____   2. _____

3. _____   4. _____

Short-term goals:

1._____

2._____

3._____

Long-term goals:

1._____

2._____

Action Plan

Strengths to be further developed and managed:

     Management:_____

     Communications:_____

     Next courses:_____

Physical actions:

     Eating habit actions:_____

     Exercise routine actions:_____

     Sleeping pattern actions:_____

Emotional actions:_____

Mental actions:_____

Spiritual actions:_____

Other actions:

     Time, energy, focus:_____

     Home life (quality time):_____

     Other activities/actions:_____

Monitoring plan:

- daily check-in
- weekly/monthly program check-in

After you complete the program, review the plan with your manager and make sure that it is right for you and the organization. If it isn't, modify the plan and make it right. Also, to ensure accountability, share your goals/actions with a partner who can help keep you accountable to your plan. The plan should be a living document and updated on at least a yearly basis.

Note for Supervisors

Employ this exercise annually on all of your staff so that you can develop them and further build program competency strengths. Recommend staff update IDPs annually for career development purposes. After the second or third year, a 360 assessment could be completed for the participant to ensure career development goals are on track. Training should be based on both individual and program needs.

SECTION 16

Communications

This section provides more details on the communication exercise participants will complete to assess how well they listen, understand the conversation, and provide direction. The purpose of this exercise is for participants to explore their effectiveness in communicating with another in a conflict situation. Note that this is a role-playing exercise that should be video-recorded so that the participant and the observers can comment on what was occurring during the discussion.

Prior to the exercise, you will need to develop different scenarios that can be discussed by two participants, with a follow-up discussion about the video. The scenario should be written out so that the participants can read the scenario prior to the session. Scenarios could be based on colleague-to-colleague dialogue, supervisor-to-employee dialogue, or employee-to-supervisor dialogue. For the first exercise, the discussion will be recorded for two minutes; for the second, three to five minutes.

A. Exercise One

In the first exercise, all participants will watch the video-recorded session and analyze the discussion: mainly, were the participants engaged in the discussion, was body language open and inviting, and did each participant feel heard? The following are feedback considerations.

Discussion follower:

- Did you understand the purpose of the discussion?
- How well did you feel heard and why?
- Did you feel like the leader was fully engaged in the discussion?

Discussion leader:

- Do you feel that you clearly stated the purpose of the communication?
- Do you feel like your body language reinforced your communication?

Observers:

- What positive actions occurred during the conversation?
- What negative actions occurred during the conversation?

B. Exercise Two

In the second exercise, you will all watch the video-recorded session and analyze the discussion. In addition to the above questions, consider the following:

- Did the individual listen, ask open questions, and give direction?
- How did the other individual feel throughout the process?
- What observations did the observers notice?
- Was it a successful conversation?
- Did it improve as compared to the first exercise?

The following are feedback considerations.

Discussion follower:

- Did you understand the purpose of the discussion?
- How well did you feel heard and why?
- Did you feel connected to the conversation?

- Did you feel motivated to act on the request?
- Did you feel like the leader was fully engaged in the discussion?

Discussion leader:

- Do you feel that you clearly stated the purpose of the communication?
- Do you feel like your body language reinforced your communication?
- Do you feel like you were effective in the conversation?

Observers:

- What positive actions occurred during the conversation?
- What negative actions occurred during the conversation?

C. Example Communication Scenarios

Following are three different scenarios that could be used as examples, or you could craft your own examples based on your experiences.

Scenario 1: Supervisor Leads the Discussion

Supervisor (Leader)
You have a senior-level employee who knows the program extremely well. In fact, this is one of your most knowledgeable employees, and you rely on this individual's abilities to help make critical program decisions. The employee has high passion for the program and excellent critical-thinking skills. The employee is very quick at reviewing different situations and quick to analyze and provide spot-on recommendations.

The employee is also very social and chatty—in a gossipy way. This individual loves to share rumors with colleagues. In fact, in meetings, the employee in many cases will dominate the conversation and take the conversation off the agenda topic. Consequently, upper-level managers have been dismissing the employee and have disinvited the employee to the different technical meetings. Additionally, colleagues have been distancing themselves from this individual.

Because of your respect for the employee and desire for the employee to succeed, you need to have a crucial conversation so that the employee is more mindful—aware—of problematic actions and the consequences they are having. Further, you want the employee to set up an action plan that will help the employee become more aware of personal communication skills so that you can have this individual participate in upper-level technical meetings.

Employee (Follower)

You are a very upbeat, social, and friendly person. You know a lot about a lot of different subjects, and you like to share your thoughts with your colleagues. You like to talk, and you dominate conversations with your colleagues.

You are also very helpful in the office. You are very intelligent and knowledgeable regarding the program. You are quick to complete high-quality products. However, when things don't go your way, you are quick to change your personality—you pout and become disengaged in your work.

You have noticed lately that you are not being invited to the senior-level technical meetings and that your colleagues are distancing themselves from you. You feel left out and want to be invited to the different meetings because you have a lot to offer. You also note that your morale is dropping as a result of the situation.

Scenario 2: Supervisor Leads the Discussion

Supervisor (Leader)

You have a senior-level employee who knows the program extremely well. In fact, the employee is one of your most knowledgeable employees, and you rely on this individual's abilities to help make critical program decisions. The employee has high passion for the program and excellent critical-thinking skills. The employee is also very quick at reviewing different situations and quick to analyze and provide spot-on recommendations.

The employee of late has been distracted from work, and overall productivity and performance are decreasing. Additionally, staff have raised concerns that this employee's disengagement in work assignments is decreasing office morale. Because of your respect for the employee, you want the employee to succeed. You need to have a crucial conversation with the employee so that the employee is more mindful—aware—of problematic actions and the consequences they are having.

Employee (Follower)

You are a very upbeat and social/friendly person. You know a lot about a lot of different subjects, and you like to share your thoughts with your colleagues. You are also very helpful in the office. You are very intelligent and knowledgeable regarding the program. You are quick to complete high-quality products. You are one of the highest performers in the office.

Recently, you ended a long-term relationship with your partner, and you are having difficulty adjusting to the situation. Consequently, you are having a hard time focusing on work, and the quality of your work is decreasing. You are stuck.

Scenario 3: Employee Leads the Discussion

Employee (Leader)

You are a very upbeat and social/friendly person. You know a lot about a lot of different subjects, and you like to share your thoughts with your colleagues. Your colleagues welcome your input. You are also very helpful in the office. You are very intelligent and knowledgeable regarding the program. You are quick to complete high-quality products. You are one of the highest performers in the office.

Additionally, you have built a great working relationship with your supervisor. Your supervisor is new and has been on the job for about six months. You and your colleagues note that your supervisor rarely promotes staff ideas or, when doing so, promotes them as the supervisor's own ideas. Staff members are frustrated.

Because of your close relationship with your supervisor, your colleagues have requested that you have a talk with the supervisor to understand why staff recommendations are not or are rarely being promoted to higher-level managers, and why there is no or limited feedback on what is moving forward.

Supervisor (Follower)

You are a relatively new supervisor within the organization. Technically, you are very skilled in your field and are internationally known for your work. As a supervisor, your skills are still developing, and you have a lot to learn as a manager. That said, you are confident in your position. Additionally, you very much enjoy coaching your staff.

However, you are uncomfortable when staff challenge your thoughts. Being relatively new to management, you also have a tendency to not inform staff of what is happening in the upper levels of management. Decisions and direction are not passed down to staff.

Scenario 4: Employee Leads the Discussion

Employee (Leader)

You are a very upbeat and friendly person. You are very intelligent and knowledgeable regarding the program. You are quick to complete high-quality products. You are one of the highest performers in the office.

Additionally, you have built a great working relationship with your third-line supervisor. Your front-line and second-line supervisors appear to be jealous of your relationship with the third-line supervisor. They continually remind you not to take advantage of the third-line supervisor's open-door policy. Further, they appear to be harder on you than other employees. They are very critical of your work products—much more so than those of others.

You are extremely frustrated with the situation and are thinking about quitting or moving into another part of the organization. Consequently, during one of your discussions with your third-line supervisor, you explain to the supervisor what you believe is happening and that you are thinking about leaving or moving to another department.

Third-Line Supervisor (Follower)

You are a relatively experienced supervisor within the organization. Technically, you are very skilled in your field and are internationally known for your work. You also very much enjoy spending time with staff and coaching them. In that light, you encourage staff to come in and discuss technical issues that they may be or are facing.

Scenario 5: Colleague to Colleague Discussion.

Colleague 1 (Leader)

You are a very upbeat person and are also very helpful in the office. You are very intelligent and knowledgeable regarding the program. You are quick to complete high-quality products. Consequently, you are assigned a lot of high-profile assignments, and you deliver on time and under budget.

You are also a team player and enjoy coaching less experienced staff. Of late, you have noticed conflict with one of your colleagues. This colleague has been very aggressive with you, and you don't understand why. Because you care about your relationship with your colleague and you know it is causing discomfort among your other colleagues, you ask your colleague to a coffee discussion to try to understand what is going on and how you can jointly move forward.

Colleague 2 (Follower)

You are a very upbeat person, and you try to be helpful in the office. You are a good employee. Unfortunately, you are not given high-profile assignments, and you want them so you can prove yourself to your supervisor. Further, you get easily frustrated when you hear about all of the good things that colleague 1 is doing. Consequently, you are expressing your frustrations to your colleagues.

Scenario 6: Colleague to Colleague Discussion.

Colleague 1 (Leader)

You are a very upbeat and friendly person. You know a lot about a lot of different subjects, and you like to share your thoughts with your colleagues. Your colleagues welcome your input. You are also very helpful in the office. You are very intelligent and knowledgeable regarding the program. You are quick to complete high-quality products. You are one of the highest performers in the office. Additionally, you have built a great working relationship with your supervisor.

However, your supervisor has betrayed you on multiple occasions, and you don't trust this individual. You don't know what to do—you like the field you are working in, and yet you know you cannot continue as things are with your supervisor. You are also uncomfortable approaching your supervisor.

You ask one of your colleagues to talk with you regarding the above situation. Note that you have a close relationship with your colleague.

Colleague 2 (Follower)

You are close to colleague 1 and know that this colleague is struggling in his/her situation. You know that this colleague wants to talk to you about the situation, but you are uncomfortable talking about it. You know that this colleague does not want to confront the supervisor, but you also you believe that this colleague needs to have that discussion. Consequently, as your colleague tries to engage you in a discussion, you continually change the topic and sidetrack the discussion. Finally, you engage in the discussion.

SECTION 17

Pretest and Posttest

This section presents the program pretest and posttest. It is recommended that the test be given during the first and last session to determine knowledge gained over the course of the program. Use the test results to determine overall success of the program. You can also use the scores to determine what materials need to be modified to ensure participants are learning the most that they can. If there are certain elements that you want to stress during the program and they are not noted below, modify the test and the materials as appropriate.

A. Test

1. **Identify the following terms with the definitions below.**
   Terms: (1) leadership and (2) supervisor

   a. Managing people: _____
   b. Managing work: _____

2. **Leadership styles (true or false):**
   a. _____ Directive/Authoritarian: Leadership is based on what is happening and/or who the individuals are.
   b. _____ Participative: This process generally affords an opportunity for employees to buy in to the process and path forward.

c. _____ Situational: Leadership is based on what is happening and/or who the individuals are.

d. _____ Transactional: A principle-centered leadership approach focused on creating a future end-state. Focus is on the "top line."

e. _____ Transformational: A leadership approach focused on accomplishing day-to-day tactical activities and based on the "bottom line."

3. **Identify the following terms with the definitions below.**
   Terms: climate, culture, goals, mission, purpose, objectives, tactics, vision

   a. _____ Specific outcomes
   b. _____ Realistic, credible, attractive future for an organization
   c. _____ The way members feel about their organization now
   d. _____ General programmatic outcomes
   e. _____ Shared attitudes, values, goals, and practices that characterize the larger institution
   f. _____ Statement of purpose that guides the actions of an organization
   g. _____ Set of actions for completion
   h. _____ Result, end, mean, aim, or goal of an action intentionally undertaken

4. **Meyers Briggs Type Indicator (MBTI) assessment is (circle the best choice):**
   a. Preference.
   b. A label.
   c. Measure of ability.
   d. Management and leadership style.
   e. All of the above.

5. **Performance (true or false):**
   a. _____ A competency model is a tool typically used for assessing your personal strengths and weaknesses.
   b. _____ Self-development plans (SDPs) should be prepared within sixty days of your start date and reviewed/revised every two years following.
   c. _____ SDPs should lay out your future goals.
   d. _____ A performance assessment should lay out the specific tasks to accommodate/accomplish your SDP.

6. **Communications: What is the preferred style of communications? (Circle the best choice.)**
   a. State issue, check your agenda, listen, summarize, address concerns, and take action.
   b. Check your agenda, state issue, listen, understand, summarize, address concerns, and take action.
   c. State issue, check your agenda, listen, understand, summarize, address concerns, and take action.
   d. State issue, check your agenda, listen, understand, summarize, and take action.

7. **Identify the following terms with the definitions below.**
   Terms: mindfulness, conflict, stress, emotional intelligence

   a. _____ is "a physical, chemical, or emotional factor that causes bodily or mental tension."
   b. _____ is "being aware" and living in the "here and now."
   c. _____ is the "ability to successfully manage yourself and the demands that you are working under."
   d. _____ is a "mental struggle resulting from incompatible or opposing needs, drives, wishes, or external or internal demands."

8. **Workforce (true or false):**
   a. _____ Lead monitoring is measuring a future outcome. For example, monitoring your fuel gage and refueling when low.
   b. _____ Lag monitoring is measuring an outcome after the fact. For example, your car stalls and you determine you ran out of gas.

9. **After-Action Reviews and Reports (true or false):**
   a. _____ AARRs are to promote learning that improves performance.
   b. _____ AARRs are always a formal process of documenting who is/who is not completing work assignments.
   c. _____ AARRs are not problem-solving processes.
   d. _____ AARRs are conducted only after an event is completed.
   e. _____ AARRs are to focus mainly on what happened, why, and how it could be done better, if repeated.
   f. _____ AARRs should be completed by the team leader.
   g. _____ AARRs are not a critique, nor do they grade success or failure.

10. **Change management: Which factors influence change? (Circle the best choice.)**
    a. Fear—real or perceived
    b. What's in it for me
    c. Power
    d. All of the above

Name   Date

Score: _____

B. Answer Key

1. **Identify the following terms with the definitions below.**
   a. Leadership (Managing people)
   b. Supervisor (Managing work)

2. **Leadership styles (true or false):**
   a. False (Directive/Authoritarian: Leadership is based on what is happening and/or who the individuals are.)
   b. True (Participative: This process generally affords an opportunity for employees to buy in to the process and path forward.)
   c. True (Situational: Leadership is based on what is happening and/or who the individuals are.)
   d. False (Transactional: A principle-centered leadership approach focused on creating a future end-state. Focus is on the "top line.")
   e. False (Transformational: A leadership approach focused on accomplishing day-to-day tactical activities and based on the "bottom line.")

3. **Identify the following terms with the definitions below.**
   a. Objectives (Specific outcomes)
   b. Vision (Realistic, credible, attractive future for an organization)
   c. Climate (The way members feel about their organization now)
   d. Goals (General programmatic outcomes)
   e. Culture (Shared attitudes, values, goals, and practices that characterize the larger institution)
   f. Mission (Statement of purpose that guides the actions of an organization)
   g. Tactics (Set of actions for completion)
   h. Purpose (Result, end, mean, aim, or goal of an action intentionally undertaken)

4. **Meyers Briggs Type Indicator (MBTI) assessment is (circle the best choice):**
   a. Best choice: Preference.

5. **Performance (true or false):**
   a. False (A competency model is a tool typically used for assessing your personal strengths and weaknesses; it is work strengths/weaknesses.)
   b. False (Self-development plans should be prepared within sixty days of your start date and reviewed/revised every two years following.)
   c. True (SDPs should lay out your future goals.)
   d. False (A performance assessment should lay out the specific tasks to accommodate/accomplish your SDP.)

6. **Communications: What is the preferred style of communications? (Circle the best choice.)**
   a. Best choice: State issue, check your agenda, listen, understand, summarize, address concerns, and take action.

7. **Identify the following terms with the definitions below.**
   a. Stress is "a physical, chemical, or emotional factor that causes bodily or mental tension."
   b. Mindfulness is "being aware" and living in the "here and now."
   c. Emotional intelligence is the "ability to successfully manage yourself and the demands that you are working under."
   d. Conflict is a "mental struggle resulting from incompatible or opposing needs, drives, wishes, or external or internal demands."

8. **Workforce (true or false):**
   a. True (Lead monitoring is measuring a future outcome. For example, monitoring your fuel gage and refueling when low.)
   b. True (Lag monitoring is measuring an outcome after the fact. For example, your car stalls and you determine you ran out of gas.)

9. **After-Action Reviews and Reports (true or false):**
   a. True (AARRs are to promote learning that improves performance.)
   b. False (AARRs are always a formal process of documenting who is/who is not completing work assignments.)
   c. False (AARRs are not problem-solving processes.)
   d. False (AARRs are conducted only after an event is completed.)
   e. True (AARRs are to focus mainly on what happened, why, and how it could be done better, if repeated.)
   f. False (AARRs should be completed by the team leader.)
   g. True (AARRs are not a critique, nor do they grade success or failure.)

10. **Change management: Which factors influence change?**
    a. Best choice: All of the above.

SECTION 18

Course Assessment

Finally, this section provides a sample program course assessment. The assessment should be used to rate the value of each session conducted in the course, the training facility, the effectiveness of the instructor, and the materials used/handed out to support the session. If results are low for a certain topic, determine what changes are necessary to improve the overall quality of the program and make those changes.

Learning Objectives

1. How did the course meet your learning objectives?
   ___ not met
   ___ partially met
   ___ fully met

Comments and recommendations:_____

2. How was the duration of the course?
   ___ too short
   ___ appropriate for materials
   ___ a little too long
   ___ too long

Comments and recommendations:_____

Russell L. Kaiser

Training Conditions

3. How do you rate training environment (room size, equipment, etc.)?
    __ poor
    __ okay
    __ good
    __ excellent

Comments and recommendations:_____

4. How well was the course organized?
    __ not well
    __ okay
    __ met expectations
    __ exceeded expectations

Comments and recommendations:_____

Overall Rating

5. How much did you learn?
    __ not much
    __ met expectations
    __ exceeded expectations

Comments and recommendations:_____

6. How useful will this course be in your daily job?
    __ not useful
    __ somewhat useful
    __ useful
    __ very useful

Comments and recommendations:_____

7. Would you recommend this course to others?
    __ no
    __ undecided
    __ yes

Comments and recommendations:_____

8. Overall rating:
    __ very disappointing; didn't meet any expectations
    __ disappointing; didn't meet expectations
    __ okay
    __ met expectations
    __ exceeded expectations

Any additional comments and recommendations:_____

9. Would you be interested in an extra session covering more topics? Yes
    or No
    If yes, which topics?_____

Session Analysis

For each of the different sessions and instructors, collect and evaluate the following information:

Session:

Presenter:

Instructor Feedback

10. How knowledgeable was the instructor/facilitator?
    __ not very
    __ okay
    __ met expectations
    __ exceeded expectations

Comments and recommendations:_____

11. Did the instructor's/facilitator's presentation support session objectives?
    __ not well
    __ okay
    __ met expectations
    __ exceeded expectations

Comments and recommendations:_____

12. How well did the instructor/facilitator answer questions from the participants?
    __ failed to address questions
    __ not well
    __ okay
    __ met expectations
    __ exceeded expectations

Comments and recommendations:_____

Presentation Materials

13. Did the presentation materials support session objectives?
    __ failed to support session objectives
    __ somewhat helpful
    __ okay
    __ met expectations
    __ exceeded expectations

Comments and recommendations:_____

14. Will you use these materials again in the future?
    __ no; will look for other sources of information
    __ maybe
    __ definitely

Comments and recommendations:_____

15. Will you recommend these materials to others?
    __ no; not helpful without following the sessions
    __ maybe
    __ definitely

Comments and recommendations:_____

Use the information provided by these responses as well as the findings from the pretest and posttest analyses to determine what potential program changes may be warranted that would make for a stronger leadership awareness and development program.

Printed in the United States
By Bookmasters